Resisting the Challenges of the 21st Century

How Much Extra Does
No Cheese Cost?

Rembert N Parker

ACKNOWLEDGEMENTS

This book never would have happened without the help and encouragement from Rembert's wife, Bevie.

Details on my journey to write and publish this book will appear in my next book, but meanwhile a big thank you is due to all the folks in the Self-Publishing School Community for all their help, without which you probably would never have found this book.

A special thanks goes out to those of you who have purchased a copy of this book. I am already working on the sequel,

Resisting the Challenges of the 21st Century, Volume 2— Nobody Wants Your Stuff

and I would like to offer you a few of the chapters from that book for free. Simply head over to

www.rembert.online/preview.htm

and supply us with an email address so we can email it to you and keep you posted about my upcoming books.

TABLE OF CONTENTS

INTRODUCTION

I grew up in a different world—the fifties. It was a time where we were expected to:

- finish school

- get a job with a company and keep it for life

- buy a car (with fins!)

- get married

- have a few kids

- buy a house and live there for forty years

- retire with a gold watch and a pension, and live out our days surrounded by friends and family.

What a crock. It's hard to believe now, but we all really believed we had a chance at that American Dream. Instead, many of us find ourselves scrambling to survive, dashing from job to job, and from relationship to relationship. Nothing seems to be permanent anymore, nothing but changes and challenges. Humor may well be our best weapon in our battle with modern life, and I will do my best to employ it here.

In this book, I will deeply examine the world we find ourselves in now. I will look at a few big problems we do not seem to be able to do much about, and at a lot of minor problems that seem even more insurmountable. I have tried to round up strands that might tie together, and divided the book into just a few sections:

- coping with modern life (because it *is* a constant struggle)

- the future (because I hope we have one)

- politics (because it just won't go away)

- television and movies (because they consume most of my free time)

- comic books and games (because I own a comic store)

- music (because I used to be a disc jockey)

If some portions seem more interesting than others, simply skip around. This book is not a novel, and while there might be a few threads that carry through the book, reappearing from time to time, each chapter should be able to stand on its own. Reading things out of order shouldn't matter very much.

Here's a bonus! I was a disc jockey at an actual radio station, and helped write and program several other radio stations later in my life, so the book has a soundtrack. There is a link at the end of each chapter that will take you to a video on YouTube that for some reason seems related to that chapter.

However, before we worry too much about the present and our future, here's a look at how I first got an inkling that I might turn out to be a writer.

PLANNING MY FUTURE—BACK IN 1962

I was attending sixth grade at West Side Elementary School in June of 1962. Our teacher was Mr. Dunham, and for the most part, I thought he was a great teacher. About a week before classes ended and we graduated to classes at Cold Spring Harbor High School, he sat on his desk, looked around at the class, and gave us one final assignment to complete.

"I want you to take out a piece of paper and write down what you expect to do for a living when you finish school," was all the direction we got from him. He then started wandering up and down the aisles in the classroom, peeking at our progress.

I sat there and gave it as much thought as I could since it was a topic I had not really spent any time on at all. The library was one of my favorite places at the school, and I had torn through all the Chip Hilton sports books and Duane Decker's stories about the Blue Sox, and those were exciting to me. Sadly, given that I had not yet had a growth spurt and was not particularly strong or fast, it was unlikely I had a future in professional sports.

Once I ran out of sports books, I had also discovered a few books by Isaac Asimov (aka Paul French) and Ray Bradbury and Arthur C. Clarke and Robert Heinlein, and continued from there to devour all the science fiction I could beg, borrow or (ahem) steal. Space exploration was even more exciting than sports, but since I nearly threw up on the Teacup ride at Disneyland, I was pretty sure physically going into space was not in my future. While fighting my way through the non-fiction stacks in the library, I had also discovered that I had an affinity for math, so working on the Space Program seemed like a reasonable future pastime. The only remaining concern was figuring out where the rockets I would be working on were going to travel.

A year earlier, the United States had put its first astronaut in space when Alan Shepard, Jr. spent a little more than 15 minutes in a suborbital flight. Almost immediately after that accomplishment, President Kennedy had declared the start of a program to put a man on the Moon, something that almost surely would happen by the end of the decade. The country had managed to put John Glenn into orbit earlier in 1962, so we were obviously on track. A little more thought and I had my future mapped out:

> In the future, I will help with the math that puts our spaceships into space. I should be deeply involved in designing the ships that can reach Mars by the end of the century and then start exploring the asteroid belt. With any luck, I will still be involved in the space program when we finally reach the moons of Jupiter.

I put my name on the page and handed it in when Mr. Dunham came around and collected the sheets.

I had no way of knowing the mistake I had made.

Mr. Dunham sat down at his desk and quickly glanced at the pages we had all written, sometimes nodding and sometimes shaking his head. His face completely changed when he got to my answer.

"Rembert, please bring another piece of paper and your pen, and come out into the hall with me." He got up and moved to the door, carrying just my sheet of paper with him.

What could I possibly have done to deserve being singled out over my carefully planned future? Once we got outside of the classroom, he carefully closed the door, and turned to me with a very disappointed look on his face. "I wanted you to take this assignment seriously. Please go down the hall and sit at one of the tables and try again. I expect better from you this time." He almost looked angry, so I quickly slinked down the hall and repositioned myself in one of the desks that lined the walls.

I do not know how long I sat there, grasping in vain for inspiration. No jobs came to mind that I did not reject immediately. I thought about falling back on professional sports, but I was pretty sure that would land me back at a desk in the hall again. I pondered several other careers, but none of them made any sense after soundly convincing myself that I needed to be working in the Space Program.

Finally, I stopped taking the assignment seriously, and then inspiration hit and I scribbled my alternate future. It did seem somewhat familiar . . .

> In the future, I will write stories about the struggles of a man who helps create the math that puts our spaceships into space. He will be deeply involved in designing the ships that can reach Mars by the end of the century and then start exploring the asteroid belt. He will struggle to live long enough and stay involved in the space program until we finally reach the moons of Jupiter.

With a definite feeling of triumph, I returned to the classroom and handed in my earliest successful writing. This time, Mr. Dunham smiled and nodded and let me take my seat again.

Three takeaways from my encounter with inspiration:

1. It is easier to sell yourself as a writer than as a rocket scientist.

2. If you are stuck for something to write about, simply sit in a quiet place all by yourself with nothing but a pen and a piece of paper and just start writing about the first thing that comes to mind. Don't worry about the results. Don't worry about selling what you have written until after you finish writing, and if you cannot sell what you have written, simply write something else.

3. In 1969, we landed on the Moon; now we probably can't even circle the Moon, let alone visit Mars. When reality lets us down, we can always write about what should have been, be it science fiction, history, or even romance.

SECTION 1:

COPING WITH LIFE
IN THE 21ST CENTURY

According to Yogi Berra, the future ain't what it used to be. Oh, sure, there are big things like no flying cars and no colonies on the moon, but it is the little things that are more like a thorn in our sides that have messed up our future. One of the things that I hate more than anything is paying for something I don't get . . .

SPECIAL NOTE FOR THE PAPERBACK
EDITION OF THE BOOK

The electronic version of the book ended each chapter with a link to a video that somehow tied to the chapter. In addition, there are still a few links embedded in this copy of the book, but you will have to key the link into a web browser to see them.

To help you out, you can go to the link shown below where the removed text and the links are waiting for you!

www.Rembert.Online/no_cheese_links.pdf

HOW MUCH DOES NO CHEESE COST?

As a kid, I used to love grilled cheese sandwiches. Nowadays, people can argue endlessly about the poor health that results from frying gobs of cheese in white bread covered with blobs of butter, and perhaps it was the heaping helping of fat that made them so attractive. Somewhere in my teens, however, dairy became a problem: if I ate butter, my tummy would start to hurt. I can still eat cheese, but as often as not, I will gag and possibly even throw up. Mercifully, eating ice cream was not **too** bad, but I rapidly developed a taste for Slurpees instead (a Slurpee was the 7-Eleven equivalent of the Icees that were common in the rest of the country). It was not long before even whole milk was a problem. If I eat cold cereal now, I tend to use 1% milk on it to minimize the misery that is probably coming later, but I tend to eat oatmeal and Cream of Wheat instead.

So it probably isn't a real surprise that I do not eat cheeseburgers. Or pizza. Or a lot of other foods most people consider to be staples of their diets. I even used to fight with my mother over getting toast that didn't have butter on it since she insisted that not putting butter on one of the pieces of toast that got cooked in the oven was a lot of extra work. It turns out my mother was not the only one who sees leaving something out as a problem; all my life, I have fought with fast food places over how I wanted my burger prepared.

Burger King made a big deal out of competing with McDonald's with the jingle, "Have it your way" since their burgers were put together on demand rather than being mass produced to be identical, but even that was a problem. Burger King used to pre-assemble their burgers by broiling the burger and putting it inside a bun with pickles and dropping that into a steaming heating bin. Since I was also not a big fan of pickles, I used to have to order a Whopper with lettuce and tomato ONLY that never had pickles on it, after which I had to watch the staff like a hawk make sure my meal get assembled properly.

I could stand a mild taste of pickles even though I did not like it, but my stomach did not want anything to do with cheese on a burger. Ordering a Big Mac with onions only and no cheese was not an easy task, and I had to all but climb over the counter sometimes to get it done right (but I did get very good at adding "and no cheese" to all my orders).

Two years ago, perhaps in an effort to boost income, Wendy's restaurants in our area made a nasty change: a single automatically became a single with cheese. After successfully getting singles with no cheese a few times, I noticed something evil: since a single without cheese was no longer on the menu, I had to pay for cheese I was not getting, adding what was, to me, a significant expense to an already expensive burger. Complaints did not help: the staff could not (or would not) argue with the computer that ran their registers, so I simply stopped eating at Wendy's (although I do get spicy chicken sandwiches from time to time when I have a coupon for buy one, get one free).

But then I had a far worse experience at Rally's. On the way to work, I noticed big posters outside the restaurant that proclaimed Rally burgers with cheese were only a dollar. I parked the car, walked up to the order window, and ordered two Rally burgers with lettuce and tomato only and no cheese. I was all set to pay when the bored employee asked me for over three dollars. In confusion, I looked around and asked if they were still on sale. The woman at the window told me that only the burgers with cheese were on sale—a Rally burger without cheese was $1.49. She even refused to hit the cheeseburger button on the register and simply turn to tell the other employee who was making the burgers to leave off the cheese.

For a moment, I was ready to channel Jack Nicholson in **Five Easy Pieces**. In the film, he tried to order toast in a restaurant, and the waitress insisted that it was not on the menu, so he could not order toast. Eventually, he ordered a chicken salad sandwich on wheat toast. No butter, no lettuce, no mayo. Moreover, when the inflexible waitress started to walk away, Jack also told her to hold the chicken salad. Poof! Toast. It did not end well.

I find it easy to believe that pieces and parts of that scene were based on multiple actual events. There was no table for me to clear, so I decided that I would leave before I got thrown out, and I probably won't return to Rally's in the near future. Taking them off my list of potential food sources is too bad because their store is located in the parking lot of the same strip center as our store. I really, really hate paying somebody for less work or fewer ingredients, so they now have one less potential customer.

NEWER MATH?

Given Donald Trump's new Secretary of Education, it seems likely that we are all about to have an encounter with the battle over Common Core. Depending on whom you listen to, it is either a step towards teaching kids to think better or a Communist plot designed to keep our children from being able to think. All the children Bevie and I produced have survived to be old enough that they will probably never face school again. It's also likely neither of us will ever have to help our grandchildren with homework (since they all live out of town), but our kids are certain to face the worst misery Common Core has to offer: Common Core Math.

Perhaps an example will illustrate the problem better than reading any of the arguments that are certain to burn up the Internet in the coming year:

How much is 345 minus 162?

Anybody who is old enough to read this book can probably do just a few "easy" calculations to answer that question:

> Five minus two is 3; 6 is bigger than four, so borrow ten, and 14 minus 6 is 8; 2 minus one is 1

The answer: 183

We can only wish that schools would teach our kids that method of doing arithmetic!

Here's Common Core Math in action:

162 to 170 is 8; 170 to 200 is 30; 200 to 300 is 100; 300 to 345 is 45;

The answer: 8 plus 30 plus 100 plus 45 is (eventually) 183

Okay, so maybe doing four little subtractions and three additions will help you understand what you are doing better than three subtractions and one addition (you carried a ten), but parents did not grow up with Common Core Math, so that will look very puzzling to them. Telling your kids to do the calculation the old way will probably even get them bad grades.

Moreover, none of that matters because all our students have calculators on their phones and can quickly click 3 4 5 − 1 6 2 = and get the right answer faster than using either method.

The irony of all this is that we fought about "understanding" math back in the sixties when the concept of "New Math" came along and blind-sided parents. The math wizards will understand it any way you present it, and everybody else will simply use their calculators—the world has changed, it is time school caught up!

Tom Lehrer's ode to New Math, written in 1962 or so illustrates the last time educators screwed around with Math. It comes complete with the line, "in the new approach, as you know, the important thing is to understand what you are doing rather than to get the right answer." Sounds like a familiar situation.

LOST AND FOUND

Another Presidential crisis has reared its ugly head. TV News, radio talk shows, and even Facebook are all full of the same old same old lately, and it reminds me of walking around stores and on campus and at friends' houses during Watergate. Everywhere you went, you were followed by the sights and sounds of Congressmen and Richard Nixon and his minions sparring over tapes. That ended, and eventually this will, too.

It is hard not to get nostalgic over some of the good things we have lost along the way, and what usually comes to mind is foods we cannot get anymore.

- Fizzies. They were these elegant little tablets that came out of a package and got dropped into a glass of water, instantly converting it into a yummy soda (think Alka Seltzer with flavors instead of over the counter medicine). Even if you did not want to drink it, there was fun to be had watching it bubble and fizz. Sadly, the flavor came from cyclamates, which caused cancer in rats that consumed truckloads of the stuff, so the FDA banned cyclamates to protect us all and Fizzies went away.

- Chocolate cigarettes. No, don't laugh, the chocolate that was in those little paper wrappers would melt in your hand before it got into your mouth if you were not fast enough, but they tasted great. That was before they put paraffin or wax or who knows what into chocolate, so it would not melt in your hand, and the taste was radically different from what we have now . . . except, possibly, the chocolate from Switzerland that costs $5 an ounce.

- Fruit Cream of Wheat. Oh, sure, they have maple-flavored Cream of Wheat still, but they used to have apple, strawberry and peach Cream of Wheat. Yes, I know they were all made with flavored apples, but still it was better than non-fruit Cream of Wheat—just search for fruit-flavored Cream of Wheat and you will find endless recipes for do-it-yourself fruit Cream of Wheat. I do not have that kind of time at 6:30 am!

- Stouffer's Roast Beef Hash came frozen and you could cook it in the oven for about a half hour (microwaves did not exist for consumers in the early seventies). You can shake your head or laugh, but it was a great meal. It was certainly better than the other frozen meals, although I do miss some of those as well. Guess they will not make meals that you cannot microwave.

- Chilitos. Taco Bell used to have Chili-Cheese Burritos, but then they went away. However, wait! The manager of our local Taco Bell drives over and picks up the special ingredients in Peru (I think there's one in Indiana . . . South America seems a tad far to travel) so they can sell them here in Anderson. Sure, they are a lot more expensive than they used to be, but at least I can still get them—no such luck with all the other foodstuffs listed here.

Wait . . . are you shaking your head at my politically incorrect diet? Too bad!

A MOST UNUSUAL SUPERBOWL

This year, the annoying Patriots beat the Falcons 34-28, and it was most unusual for all sorts of reasons. The ones everybody is zeroing in on are pretty simple:

- The first Superbowl where a team overcame a deficit of 14 points or more and won.

- The first time a quarterback won five or more Superbowls.

- The first Superbowl that went into overtime.

However, the game stood out for a few more reasons:

- A portion of the half-time was secretly prerecorded (Lady Gaga on the roof). We have had Superbowl half-times where they lip-synced to prerecorded music, but the drones used in the program could not be over the stadium during the game, so they recorded the start of the show a week early. I will not even mention the first use of drones in a half-time show because the NSA might have been doing that for years.

- The final score was within one touchdown. Counting manually, I found that only 16 of the 51 Superbowls had final scores where the winner won by less than 7 points.

- The ads were not very good. The poor ads were the major disappointment for me.

The last item is the one that surprised me. For years, I have been recording the Superbowl while I watched something else I already had recorded, and after each one hour show ended (about every 42 minutes) I would fast forward through the plays and watch the commercials. Unfortunately, the Internet has killed Superbowl commercials. The ads have become so expensive ($5 million per thirty seconds plus the cost of making the ads) that companies struggle to get their money's worth. Many of the companies posted their ads to YouTube a week or so before the big game. There were even websites posting lists and links for the ten best ads days before the Superbowl. The lack of surprises probably helped make the ads seem even less impressive than they already were.

The one big mystery was the live ad, but they did such a poor job on the ad that most people did not notice it, didn't realize what it was an ad for, and probably don't even remember it—sorry, Snickers.

I thought the Budweiser immigrant ad was good, but Bevie was annoyed that the only Clydesdales in the ad were two horses in the background of one quick shot. The ghost of Spuds Mackenzie was not a good replacement for the horses (and sorry for all the youngsters who do not have a clue about who Spuds was).

There were more than a few ads that concentrated more on being politically correct than on humor, and for the most part, people simply seemed to be tired of that. Seriously, who thought it was a good idea to alienate half the audience by being political on either side of the fence?

My favorite ad was turned down by Fox—the ad for 84 Lumber. Fox only showed a modified version of the ad that they thought wouldn't be as controversial (they replaced a wall with a fence) and cut off the actual ending. You can probably still find the complete ad online.

BEGGARS—CAN—BE CHOOSERS

Now that our family has mostly moved into retirement, over half of our income comes from running a small business, a comic and game store. Since income from that is erratic, we do not know how much income we will have from month to month. As a result, we base our budget for some things on how much money we have left at the end of the month. While we can usually send at least some money to Second Harvest to help provide food to the food banks that supply food to people who desperately need it, any other charitable giving is totally dependent on our cash flow that month. Moreover, yes, that does mean some months there is no extra money.

During the month, we get the usual snail mail asking us to please send money. Actual bills get paid since about half of our income is fixed and we can budget such things, but during the month, I sort through the mail soliciting money and I stack them up until the end of the month.

We were both born in the fifties, so we're still enjoy getting actual physical magazines in the mail and reading them while we pay half-attention to the television, and magazine subscriptions usually go on the stack. Our limit is usually about ten dollars a year for a magazine subscription, or maybe 50 cents an issue for magazines that come out more frequently than monthly. I am pretty sure that barely covers the cost of shipping the magazines to us, but the magazine companies make their money off the ads we ignore. I even have two subscriptions that are permanent—for as long as I live, the magazines will continue to come for free. I missed out on the best deal ever for magazines: apparently, Time magazine sold permanent subscriptions back in the thirties or so. If you were lucky enough to buy one of those subscriptions, you can designate a successor to receive the future magazines, and they can name a successor, ad infinitum. My lifetime subscriptions have mostly been a good idea, although one of the other magazines I had that sort of subscription to went out of business and a fourth went digital only.

Yesterday, we got a letter from a charity we have sent money to from time to time that looked familiar, but closer inspection revealed some changes to the form they sent us. As usual, the form they wanted back had boxes to pick the amount of our gift, starting at $25 and going higher from there. In the past, there was always a box marked "Other" that I could check so I could send a smaller amount, but not this time. Further, while there were all the necessary lines to enable a credit card payment, there was no box to x out for "My Check Is Enclosed." Further examination of the enclosed materials showed comments related to "Renewal of your gift" and "Change the frequency of your gift."

Huh? They are no longer interested in communicating with people who want to send them a check once in a while? Was there some fine print somewhere in all that paper that was setting us up for a monthly donation on our credit card automatically?

Confused, and disappointed, I ripped up the mailing and dropped it into the trash instead of putting it on the stack for consideration at the end of the month. If nothing else, we can send extra money to Second Harvest this month.

ANYTHING BUT CASH

I got my first debit card in 1971. The insurance company I worked for owned the bank on the street level of their building, and they distributed debit cards to everybody. I vaguely recall cancelling it and cutting it up into little pieces within a year or so because the bank downstairs was convenient enough that getting cash was easy. I really did not need the card. While my habits have not changed all that much, the world has beaten a path to the credit/debit card door. Moreover, those knocking on the door are having the floor open up underneath them and dump them into transactional hell: welcome to the age of the chip card.

Chip cards are simply credit or debit cards that come with something special. In addition to the magnetic strip on the back of the card, the chip cards have a coppery square on the front that has an integrated circuit. Most U.S. citizens think that the chip cards are new, but the store has had a machine that could read the chips for more than eight years, and chips of one sort or another have been around since France introduced them in 1986.

Wikipedia on EMV cards:
https://en.wikipedia.org/wiki/EMV

The formats of the circuits on the chips have changed over time. As used in Europe (and Canada, and Australia, and pretty much any country with any sense) the user plugs their chip into a machine and enters a pin. The pin is usually just four numbers, but in some places they use six.

The box takes the chip information and the pin and produces a one-time use code. The information sent out for the transaction does not include the account number or the pin or anything else useful. The net result is much better security since there is no easy way to copy the information and reuse it.

In the United States? Apparently, the card companies (or the banks) don't believe we can remember a four digit code, so the default is putting the chip into the machine and getting a signature. Sadly, the signature is often put into the machine and never shown to a human, so it is no security at all—if somebody steals your chip credit card, they can use it in most places without fear. Banks that issue debit cards have the option to require a pin, and based on our problems in the store, more and more of them are doing so.

The problems created by the chips are overwhelming! The first time I used a chip card at Wal-Mart, it took nearly five minutes of standing around while I waited for the transaction to be approved. A week or so later when I went back again using the chip was as fast as swiping, so no doubt Wal-Mart spent some big bucks to solve that problem. We have seen similar problems at our store with some cards that take forever but eventually work. We have seen cards that take forever and then don't work with strange error messages. We have seen some cards that don't work at all. We have even had cards work quickly and easily on our machine that **wouldn't** work that morning at Wal-Mart or Meijer, so the problems are many and varied. Some stores still won't let you use the chip, requiring customers to swipe the card. Our machine will not let us swipe a card that has a chip (we just get a message that says, "Use chip reader").

So why are stores still fighting to find ways to use the chip cards if they cause so much trouble? Blackmail! If a customer swipes a card that has a chip, the merchant is at risk instead of the credit card company or the bank when fraud is involved with a stolen card. The consumer using the card is still safe, but the retailer gets kicked to the side of the road and held down while the credit card company liberates money from the pockets of the poor retailer. Expect more troubles to continue into the foreseeable future, followed by everybody somehow accepting the chip cards. However, watch out for crooks scanning the cards in your pocket that use radio transmissions to make transactions from a distance. The only protection from that is a wallet with a special lining.

TO CANADA, EH?

For a multitude of reasons, I rarely mail things to Canada, but now and then, I do not have much choice. Sending a letter to Canada used to be simple: write the letter, put it in an envelope, place a stamp on the envelope, drop it in any mailbox. Of course, that was back when stamps all had numbers on them: 4 cents, 5 cents, 6 cents, 8 cents, 10 cents . . . notice a pattern? Those numbers keep getting larger over time (I am assuming no readers were alive in 1919 when prices somehow managed to decrease). Stamps now cost nearly 50 cents each (I think) but there's a major difference: no numbers!

From time to time (but not as often as we remember) the post office has increased the price of a one ounce letter. I have a vague feeling that Congress (or somebody in the government) has to approve the increases, and at times, the Post Office may not get the increase they hope to get. Back in 1975, the Post Office was trying to get an increase in postage rates. They had to order the printing of millions of stamps before the rate hike they requested was approved, so somebody got the bright idea of printing the stamps with the letter "A." Once the rate was approved, stamps with the letter A were good for mailing a 13 cent letter, even though the letters sent before that were only 10 cents. We will table a discussion of the brutal inflation of the late seventies for another time.

The letter A stamps worked fine for a few years, but in 1977, the postal rate jumped to 15 cents, and that price hike created a new problem. Oh, sure, printing stamps with the letter B while the Post Office waited for a new rate hike to be approved worked fine, but it created a real problem for millions or tens of millions or hundreds of millions of letters. An A stamp was not enough postage anymore, and Americans faced with an unusual shortage: the Post Office rapidly ran out of two cent stamps since people needed one of them for every letter they wanted to send with an A stamp. The Post Office finally eliminated the complication of letter stamps when Forever Stamps were issued in 2007, although you can still use your old letter stamps. Do you want to confuse a poor mail carrier? Send out a letter with combinations of an A stamp, a B stamp, a C stamp, a D stamp, and maybe another small stamp to get up to full postage.

The letter stamps had another, unintended consequence: Canada was unwilling to accept the letter stamps because there was no telling how much a stamp was worth. The confusion might have come from the exchange rates (but part of it might have been the confusion caused by A stamps and Eh stamps). As a result, letters sent to Canada had to have actual cents printed on them. Getting stamps with prices on them became increasingly difficult, but the post office had a way around that: the US International stamp. Sure, it is expensive ($1.15 right now), but it lets you mail a letter out of the country, currently using a surprisingly beautiful stamp.

THE MANDELA EFFECT

If you were around in the late 1960s, you might remember when "news" broke that Paul McCartney had died and the Beatles replaced him with somebody who looked a lot like him. Lots of pieces of "proof" showed up as people played Beatles records backwards, studied album photos, and searched for photos of Paul in the media. There was almost mass hysteria on campus because of the feeling that somehow our reality had been changed without our knowledge.

That was nothing—meet the Mandela Effect.

About a half-dozen years ago, Fiona Broome and a second, unnamed person had a discussion at DragonCon where they discovered that they both vividly remembered Nelson Mandela dying in prison, including some hints of the memory of watching his funeral on television. These memories are questionable in the face of "facts" since Mandela came out of prison, became president of South Africa, and was still alive for a time after that (in current reality, he died three or four years later). What impressed those two was how closely their individual memories matched each other, even though reality had different ideas about what had happened.

As a result of that chance conversation, Fiona started questioning other people about Mandela, and discovered that while most people "correctly" identified Mandela as still alive, a significant number of people had the same memories of his death and funeral. Once she had that information, Fiona had her eyes opened to other possibilities, and she unearthed a slew of similar shared, conflicting memories. She started a website in 2010 to follow up on what she termed The Mandela Effect.

It has been a half a decade since that breakthrough, but discussions of the effect have, as Fiona notes, reached the tipping point and there are lots and lots and lots of articles starting to appear online about the Mandela Effect

Other examples?

"Mirror, mirror on the wall, who's the fairest of them all?" Nope, that was not in the movie.

Berenstein Bears. Nope, it is the Berenstain Bears (the "correct" version simply looks wrong to me).

On which eye does the rich tycoon in the Monopoly game wear his monocle? Answer: neither. He does not even **have** a monocle!

There are lots of websites (and many videos) that investigate the Mandela Effect, but nobody has a good explanation for it. Well, Fiona does, but it is difficult to prove. She posits that there are lots of alternative realities in parallel worlds, and somehow, we can travel between them and take some of our memories with us (even though most of our memories get "converted"). Some people have even suggested that time travel might be possible using this kind of reality hopping.

Is the Mandela Effect any more real than Paul's death? Alternatively, was Paul's death simply an early example of the Effect? A person can spend days wandering around the web, reading all about it and not come to any conclusions (yet).

DOWNLOADING AT 0 KB/S

A recent span of a few short weeks was a tough time for my computers. Microsoft sent through an update to Windows 10 on Friday night, and everything seemed to be okay, but when I came back on Saturday morning, the computer simply refused to boot.

When I finally got the computer back to the store that built it a few years ago, they insisted that there was no way to salvage anything, and proceeded to rebuild Windows 10 (charging me extra since I could not find my serial number). All my files? Gone.

Well, there was always my backup computer, but it stopped responding, too. The power supply went bad, and the old version of Windows that was on it refused to reboot or reload, so I had to install Windows 10 on that computer as well.

Now, I do have backups for things that matter, but it turns out many things are not easily backed up:

- all my browser saved places

- all the passwords Chrome had saved for me

- all the "valuable" information saved in cookies

- all the information that various programs stored who knows where (player id numbers and, sadly, all my tax files—I must fall back on printed copies)

- all the information YouTube had saved about what I liked to listen to (since I almost never log in to YouTube, information is saved "somewhere" on my hard drive, but not in the cloud or on YouTube itself)

The worst problem turns out to be the browser saved places. Many of those addresses are "secrets" that are passed along to us by manufacturers and distributors and such, and replacing those can even require emails back and forth. I probably still haven't recovered all of them.

The second worst problem is reloading "applications". Not just the easy ones (Chrome and a PDF reader), but also the anti-virus software I always want to download before I dare download anything or wander the web. Moreover, of course, Office is gone. Again.

This morning, I pushed the power button and the computer whirred for a while and then sat there. I powered down and tried again, and still nothing. The fourth try seemed to work, but Windows announced that the reboot had failed, and insisted on reinstalling Windows 10 again all by itself. At least this time, it was nice enough to let me keep my files. But not my browser or its saved places or my passwords.

So I started downloading my anti-virus software and Office and . . . it has not been pleasant. The applications show not only their progress at downloading, but also the download speed. The maximum my ISP seemed to be willing to grant me was a puny 180 kilobytes per second, but after a while, the Internet seemed to run out of gas, and my speed dropped and dropped and dropped. And it finally reached a completely unimpressive 0 kb/s.

WE KNOW WHO'S *NOT* COMING TO DINNER

With all the problems our country faces, it almost seems like an April Fool's joke that we spent so much time worrying about whom Vice President Pence will and won't eat dinner with. Last week, his wife revealed that Pence will not eat dinner alone with another female and will not attend events where alcohol is served unless his wife is with him. For some reason, far too many people got upset about this, carrying on and on about how this reveals something weak or suspicious about the Vice President.

I assume the Vice President will also avoid closed-door meetings alone with a female as well, and that I completely understand.

At one of the jobs I had in the past, I would sometimes meet with people in my office with the door closed. It did not matter if they were male or female, whether the topic was a performance review or a confidential discussion, I would simply close the door. Closing the door did not raise any red flags and nobody ever suggested that there might be anything improper about a closed-door meeting.

At another job, even before I started work, I was advised that at no time was I to close the door to my office when there was only one female in the room. There had apparently been some unacceptable behavior on the part of a previous occupant of that office, and the employer did not want a repeat performance. I simply ignored that suggestion when the other person in the room was my wife.

Why the reason for the difference in the rules for the two jobs? While some readers might jump to an assumption that the employers were modern sophisticates in one case and medieval conservatives in the other (like some of the conclusions about Pence), there was a significant difference in the two offices: windows. In the first office, I had windows all the way across the room that started about three feet from the floor and went all the way to the ceiling. Even with the door closed, a dozen or more people could see into the office at all times. The second office had a solid wall and a solid door that, when closed, sealed off the office from view.

Not only did keeping the door open in the second office prevent even the appearance of impropriety, but it also helped prevent accusations of impropriety.

I have had meals with coworkers and my supervisors any number of times, and never had any qualms about that situation. I can understand how other people would be uncomfortable when faced with the potential problems that could arise from having a meal alone with somebody who reported to them. Anymore, it is difficult to know when people might construe such a meal as unintended or even intentional sexual harassment due to the power dynamic of such a situation. It is entirely possible that the Vice President came to his current limitations on dining as a result of his work as a congressman and governor and the need to avoid potential scandals.

Not attending events where there is alcohol without his wife? Maybe that goes back to a promise he made a few decades ago. I cannot even begin to figure that one out, but worrying about that seems even less constructive. I will smile, however, at the Vice President's comment when he gave a speech the next week: "Speaking of my wife, Karen, she is really sorry she couldn't be with us today, she already had dinner plans." We can only assume nobody was openly drinking alcohol at that dinner.

WHY WE ARE PLAYING MUSICAL CHAIRS ON OUR AIRPLANES

The news has been full of problems related to seating passengers on airplanes recently. This week's problem arose when a family tried to fly back to the mainland from Hawaii. I have been reading various accounts of the situation, and believe I have finally solved the mystery of what happened and who's to blame. While the conclusions of this article are conjecture on my part, it relies on pieces and parts of other news reports.

While nobody was beaten or trampled this time, it does sound ominous: the family with three tickets had strapped a car seat in place and put their 2-year-old son into the car seat. They were also traveling with a 1-year-old baby that was in their lap. They were then told that they could not use the safety seat and had to hold their child in somebody's lap during the entire flight. The family agreed to hold the 2-year-old during takeoff, but insisted on being allowed to put the child back in the seat after that.

There is a video on YouTube of the nightmare that followed. Things escalated, and it appears that a Delta supervisor came on board and told the family that FAA restrictions required the child to remain in somebody's lap the entire flight. Threats of putting the parents in jail and taking their children away followed. Fortunately for all concerned, the family eventually deplaned peacefully. Expenses of over $2,000 resulted from spending another night in Hawaii and booking passage back to California the next day (no doubt on a different airline).

At the very least, Delta needs to retrain the person who confronted the family. FAA restrictions do **not** require children under 2 to sit on somebody's lap. In fact, according to KTLA,

> The FAA issued a statement to KTLA that the agency's safety regulations encourage parents to secure children in a separate seat "in an appropriate restraint based on weight and size."

> "The safest place for a young child under the age of two on an airplane is in a child restraint, not on a parent's lap," the FAA statement read.

Even Delta's website agrees with that sentiment:

> We want you and your children to have the safest, most comfortable flight possible, for kids under the age of two, we recommend you purchase a seat on the aircraft and use an approved child safety seat.

So what happened here? It turns out that the family's 18-year-old son had traveled with them on the flight to Hawaii during which they placed the child and the safety seat on an empty seat. The family bought a ticket to send the son back to California the day before the rest of the family flew back. I do not know many 18-year-olds who would leave Hawaii a day early! It was the family's intention to use the unused ticket for his seat the next day for the child seat.

One radio report mentioned that the family had not paid to change the name or date of the ticket for the 18-year-old, and that points us towards a possible explanation of what was going on.

The family appeared to have only three tickets for the round trip. On the flight to Hawaii, there must have been empty seats available so they could again place the child on an empty seat. Instead of simply buying a ticket for the extra seat on the flight back, the family bought a one-way ticket for their son to return early—a step that only makes sense if the flight back was full. The airline insisted that the plane was not oversold, but it probably *was* sold out.

When the family checked in at the gate, the 18-year-old did not check in because he was already back in California, and a computer switched his ticket to a no-show before the plane got ready for take-off.

Since there was a no-show, somebody who wanted to fly back early or who was on stand-by immediately bought the seat. Delta then faced the prospect of two passengers wanting to use the same seat: the family (which had a now-invalid ticket) and the new person who was holding a valid boarding pass. To their credit, the airline tried to resolve the problem by placing the child back in a parent's lap, but the family was not amused: they had paid for a ticket on that plane, and expected to use the seat.

The main problem? Tickets tend to be non-transferrable and non-changeable. If customers were allowed to buy tickets and transfer them to somebody else, you would never be able to buy a cheap advance ticket again. Instead, some company would figure out how they could make money by buying up ALL the cheap seats on flights that were likely to be full and reselling them to desperate

36

passengers closer to the flight time. At MUCH higher prices. That would be a terrible result.

Perhaps the family could have paid a fee to transfer the 18-year-old's ticket to a different flight and pay for a ticket for the safety seat, and that might even have been an option had they discussed it with the airline. Perhaps Delta could have handled the transfer of the seat to a different child for a fee when the family arrived at the airport. Perhaps things could have been worked out, but they could not be because of the culprit in all this.

It's because of the computer system. As soon as the computer had the information that there was a no-show for the flight, it sold the seat. After that, there was no way for Delta to recover. So blame Skynet.

SECTION 2:

THE FUTURE

What, no flying cars? That's okay, nobody predicted computer games or phones that are even close to what we already have!

APPLYING AUGMENTED REALITY

Last year saw the rise of Pokémon Go, an app that allows people to look at their surroundings through their phone's camera and see Pocket Monsters that obviously aren't there in the real world. The app communicates with a database that is updated almost constantly and shows specific Pokémon in specific locations. Many people decided this was lots of fun, and it caused a surprising number of people to get out of their homes and walk around outside and even talk and laugh with strangers.

Great idea.

Adding unreality to reality through a database, a communication device, and a monitor (in this case, a phone or tablet) made for a great game and is referred to as Augmented Reality. Looking at the phone lets you see more than the reality that is there, it augments reality by adding to it.

An app that was written to help people find the exact location of nearby creatures succeeded in breaking the game by making it easier to find the creatures, and the game designers ended up blocking the app that did that. Many players stopped the game when they lost their favorite cheating app.

Fortunately, there are better ways to use Augmented Reality. That first struck me when I had to visit a doctor in an unfamiliar hospital. The almost helpful people at the reception counter gave me what sounded like reasonable directions. It turned out those directions only made sense to somebody who already knew where they were going. I ended up having an amused worker bee all but take me by the hand and lead me through the maze of the hospital and drop me off at the doctor's office. We will not talk about my trip out of there. Sure, there were colored lines on the floor, but I had to follow a line for a while, then follow another line, then switch buildings, and it just didn't work out well. It would have been a lot easier for me if they had simply given me a map I could orient.

An even better approach came to mind. What if there were an app you could download that would interface with the hospital's database and produce an augmented reality creature that would trot down the hallways and lead me to the office? For a small fee, I could even switch to following Dr. McCoy from Star Trek, or Nurse Ratched from One Flew over the Cuckoo's Nest or maybe even Pikachu until I reached my goal. The guide would always show up in front of me when I faced the direction I needed to go, so if I started going the wrong way, I could simply look around with my phone until I saw my guide, and then start walking in the correct direction again.

Just think, never get lost in the woods again, either, because Davy Crocket will be there to lead you back to camp.

But, wait, there's more! Need something specific in a grocery store or Wal-Mart? Just type it into your phone and the app will pop up an imaginary shopping cart that leads you there. Figuring out the shortest path to visit a series of locations is easy to solve. You can make a list of items you want to find (using the store's app before you get there, no doubt offering you coupons and such to change your list) and when you arrive, your phone will lead you down the shortest (or quickest) route to pick up all your items.

Shucks, an app like that would make it easy for Amazon to fill up a box with all the books, seeds, games and vitamins you ordered without anybody having to spend too much time looking at numbers on the shelves and wandering around endless aisles of inventory, wondering where to look next.

So, there you have it, today's billion-dollar idea. Implementation is left as an exercise for the reader.

WHERE TO FIND A FIDUCIARY
(AND WHY YOU NEED TO)

This chapter is all about you saving and investing money so that when you get old, you still have some money. Be serious for a second, how much do you trust Social Security in the future? You should not rely on this article for tax or accounting or legal information; consult your own experts for that—this article is mostly about trying to steer you to get some help.

The easiest or best way to save and invest for the future is through a 401(k) or IRA. If you work for a non-profit company, you might be offered a 403(b) plan, which is like the 401(k). I will refer to both of these plans as simply 40x plans. There's a rapidly diminishing chance that you work somewhere that offers a pension since those retirement programs are disappearing.

A 40x plan is usually set up by your employer; in good plans, the employer matches some of your savings by adding some money to your savings. As an extra incentive, your investments grow tax-free as long as you do not take any money out of them before age 60 or so. You either get to avoid taxes on the money you put in (regular 40x plans) or get to take money out without paying any taxes (the relatively new Roth 40x plans; the money that resulted from your employer's contributions to a Roth plan will probably still be taxable).

If you do not have an employer with a 40x plan, you can open your own IRA and achieve pretty much the same results. If you are self-employed, you can create a special Simplified Employee Pension (SEP) with a one-page form and some help from a bank or brokerage firm.

As an alternative to any of these options, you can always invest money without using a tax shelter, but then you will have the opportunity to pay lots of income taxes through the years.

In the past, retirement accounts were set up by insurance companies, banks, or brokerage firms. Companies typically charged you fees and compensated the people who "helped" set up and administer those accounts by paying them commissions. The fees they charged you could be a percentage of your deposits and/or fixed monthly or annual charges. It was not unusual for the fees to reduce your earnings dramatically. If your company's retirement plan was set up by a broker or insurance agent, your employer might have paid some of the fees, but the fees almost always hammered your account as well. Since commissions could vary a great deal from contract to contract, this put the people receiving the commissions in a bad situation. They had to decide, should they sell your company a plan that charges 5% fees and pays them a 5% commission on all investment monies or sell your company a plan that charges 1% fees and pays only a 1% commission?

Maybe they would compromise and find a plan with 3% fees and only 3% commissions. Maybe not. Would you voluntarily take an 80% pay cut, simply to help out a client who would probably never notice? Sure you would.

Every financial advisor faces this built-in conflict between what is best for their client and best for their own income.

In the past, the most financial advisors had to worry about was placing clients in investments that met a suitability test. Any investments had to be reasonable, but they did not have to be the best possible investments for the client. The suitability test allowed advisors to recommend plans with higher fees that paid higher commissions without putting any pressure on them to save their customers' money.

The Obama administration tried to help out by setting in place a regulation that would require financial advisors who dealt with any retirement plan to have a fiduciary relationship with their clients. This relationship would require that they act only in their client's best interest, which would make it more difficult for the advisors to justify plans with high expenses and high commissions.

One way to solve the problem is for financial advisors to charge a fee for their advice instead of receiving commissions or other compensation, after which they would look for the best possible plan for their customers. The problem with that approach is how expensive it is to talk with an advisor (expect to pay $50 to $250 an hour for their expertise). One reason the fiduciary requirement was controversial is that it would make it more difficult for investors with small amounts of money and little money to pay for time with an advisor to get any advice for their situation. One hope was that employers would pay for classes where advisors would help their employees.

Paying extra fees does not sound like a problem for you? Okay, suppose you have $100 a month to invest from age 25 to age 65 (we will ignore both raises and inflation). Did you want to face retirement with $73,443 that will all be fully taxable when you withdraw it or with $632,407 that will all be tax-free? A financial advisor with a suitability requirement can place you in either of those results with no consequences (except higher income for them with the first plan). Having a fiduciary relationship with somebody whose primary concern is your well-being might be important.

The Trump administration has already started trying to remove the fiduciary requirement before it even gets in place. Many places online will recommend that you look for financial advisors that voluntarily set up a fiduciary relationship with you, but they will no doubt be difficult to find. Fortunately, there is a way for you to find a financial advisor who will only have your best interest in mind:

> The best way to find a financial advisor with a fiduciary relationship to you is to look in the mirror.

Sure, relying on yourself will require you to study up on investing, but that is not difficult—there are stacks of books at the library or on Kindle, and reading several of them is better than reading just one. If you must set up your own retirement vehicles, there are plenty of brokerage firms that will set up accounts with few or no fees. If you need special help with your situation, there are experts you can consult on an hourly basis who can supply the guidance you need, and having at least an annual meeting with an advisor will probably help you identify your goals and keep you on track to reach them.

More and more, it is becoming clear that passive investing with just four low fee investment instruments (ETFs) will usually outperform almost any actively managed investment vehicle with far less risk. Go read up on them.

THE UNINTENDED CONSEQUENCES OF AUTOMATION

Back in 1982, I was working in the basement of a Credit Company, one of a few dozen people working in their insurance subsidiary. Most of what they sold was credit insurance that was related to the loans they made in their credit offices. The company also sold whole life policies which developed some cash values, which in turn produced the possibility of paid-up insurance and/or extended insurance. The amount of coverage for these rather small policies was based on the premium, and as a result, the cash values for the policy were based on the face amount the premium could buy. State Insurance Departments required the policies to contain the actual cash values that would be available, which meant that somebody had to calculate the cash values based on the face amount and the issue age (and probably the sex and maybe the smoking habits).

There was a bank of young women whose job it was to multiply the face amount (divided by 1000) times at least 25 numbers and then type those numbers onto a page that they would then insert into the policy. At that point, the policies would move into my office and become my worry. I was responsible for checking all the numbers they typed to make sure those numbers were correct.

Ouch. Why didn't somebody warn me about that during the job interviews?

When my job started, I was still staying at a nearby hotel, watching all of four or five channels on the pitiful excuse the hotel had for television. Since my first few weeks at the job were pretty busy, I took those policies back to the hotel with me and checked them for correctness.

It only took one night of checking policies before I tried talking with somebody, anybody in the data processing department in hopes of getting a computer program in place to do away with the drudgery of creating those policy pages and, more importantly, checking them. It turned out that the data processing department had nothing but a mainframe, and their programming staff was simply much too busy for something as trivial as printing policy pages, so maybe they would consider it in a few months. One estimate was 18 months, so I suggested to my boss that we spend some money to buy a microcomputer to automate the pages. He did not seem too interested in solving a problem that no longer required him to check policy pages.

Undaunted (and tired of multiplying numbers in my calculator and checking them against stacks of paper), the next weekend I returned to my soon-to-be ex-home. I packed up my trusty TRS-80 Model I and brought it back to the hotel. It only took about an hour to create a program to print the policy pages after you entered a few pieces of information. The next night, I spent a few hours keying in all the numbers you could ever possibly need to print those pages. I triumphantly took the computer to my office the following day and let my boss know that if he would simply spend about $1,500, we could make the pages easier to produce and much more dependably correct without any unnecessary checking. Faced with a completed system, he decided computerization was an excellent idea. We had a TRS-80 Model III in the office shortly after that (the Model

I could only show 64 columns on the mono-color screen, but the Model III had a card that supported a full 80 columns!) The data processing department was not pleased, but they were too busy to worry about the encroaching microcomputer.

And about a week later, there were at least a half-dozen fewer employees in our area. It turns out that with a microcomputer calculating and printing all the numbers, it just took a couple of the more intelligent young women who could deal with a computer to do all the work that the entire area was doing before (at least those few who remained got minor raises).

I had assumed that the company would simply transfer the existing employees and give them something else to do. Instead, it turned out that the company felt their best option was to save money by terminating most of the clerical workers who had been doing all the manual work. In penance, I spent the next two years writing programs that ran on the mainframe that replaced most of my job. After that, I left and went back to college and learned to build neural networks while I prepared to teach computer programmers (although I would not finish a masters for another 20 years . . . and I completed a doctorate a handful of years after that).

That was close to the beginning of a wave that is about to crash on the shore of our economy, drowning countless jobs under an endless supply of artificial intelligence, neural networks, and automation. For the lucky few who have whatever skills turn out to be necessary, jobs will be plentiful . . . for everybody else, not so much.

While companies will replace the taxi and truck drivers with self-driving vehicles, somebody will probably still have to ride along in the trucks or supervise the taxis and deal with problems that arise. As computers learn to read MRIs better than humans do, somebody else will still need to load the MRIs into the machines and do something with the results. Until the computers can program themselves, somebody will still need to tell them what to do. However, the number of jobs for computer professionals will probably peak in another decade or two and then start to decline as we run out of things to automate.

On the other hand, Mr. Roboto may have an easier time finding work.

SECTION 3:

POLITICS

Whose idea *was* politics, anyway? Lately, it seems to be little more than a way to separate us from each other rather than a way to solve the common problems we face.

HOW TO SPEND OTHER PEOPLE'S MONEY

A long time ago advertisers discovered that one way to get the attention of viewers was to use popular songs in their ads. Using the music for ads usually makes money not for the groups that created the songs, but rather for the owner of the publishing rights. Figuring out who owns the publishing rights to a song can sometimes be a surprise.

Back in 1985, Michael Jackson outbid Paul McCartney and bought Associated Television Corporation's publishing assets, including songs from the Beatles. McCartney fumed, but couldn't do much about it, and almost immediately, we started to hear Beatles music in ads. A fortunate change in the copyright laws means that Paul is currently on his way to getting those rights back, after which we likely won't hear any more misplaced Beatles music (although we all know that somewhere down the line, his heirs will probably sell or license the rights).

Some artists have been fortunate enough to keep hold of their publishing, leading to defiant stands by musicians like Neil Young, whose song **This Note's for You** makes it very clear that he is not interested in hearing his songs in commercials (check the lyrics if you are not familiar with the song). The song got Neil nominated for a Grammy, but he lost out to Weird Al's song, **Fat**, a very funny take-off of Michael Jackson's **Bad**. To come full circle on the irony of all that, MTV allegedly wouldn't initially show the video for **This Note's for You** because it included a clip that made fun of Michael Jackson's hair catching fire when he was working on an ad for Pepsi.

However, today, a third way to deal with your publishing rights was declared by Grace Slick, the lead singer of Jefferson Airplane and later Jefferson Starship (aka just Starship for the song in question after the threats of a lawsuit). Chick-fil-A wanted to use the Starship song, **Nothing's Gonna Stop Us Now** in an ad. Publishing rights resided with Grace, so it was up to her to either allow the usage (for a fee) or tell Chick-fil-A to use somebody else's property.

The decision is not as simple as take the money or don't take the money—the founder of Chick-fil-A has donated much money to organizations that worked very hard to oppose gay marriage, so Grace's initial thought was to decline the opportunity. However, after giving the matter a second thought, she came up with a better idea: she accepted the offer (nobody knows how much money is involved) and donated all the money she got to Lambda Legal:

> Lambda Legal, a 501(c)(3) nonprofit, is a national organization committed to achieving full recognition of the civil rights of lesbians, gay men, bisexuals, transgender people and everyone living with HIV through impact litigation, education and public policy work.

Nice way to work with other people's money!

GET OUT OF OUR PARK . . .
AND TAKE YOUR POKÉMON WITH YOU

Back in the dark ages known as the 1970s, the police in Nashville decided to fight crime the best way they could think of: they arrested people in Centennial Park for a heinous crime. The park is located about two or three blocks from Vanderbilt University. It is a lot more elaborate now, but at the time, it was mostly a long expanse of grass which surrounded several useful parts of the park.

The center of the park contains the Parthenon, a full-scale model of the Athenian Parthenon in Greece. There are several pieces of sculpture there, and no doubt those of an artistic bent can wander around marveling at the pieces (once through is more than enough for me).

There's also a small artificial "lake" (looks more like a pond to me). Maybe you can fish there, maybe you cannot, but it is certainly cooler by the lake in the shade of the trees than walking around on the sidewalks.

There's a staging area as well. I have vague memories of seeing free concerts there, including such notables as Brian Hyland near the end of his hit record period and Grand Funk Railroad when they were barely getting started.

Overall, not a bad place to spend time. At least, not until the police started to arrest people. For Loitering. In a park. During the daytime. Really? Fortunately, the judge that had the cases presented to him had enough sense to throw the cases out and reprimand the police. Newspaper articles let on that the park had become a hotbed for drug deals, and the police were just trying to crack down on that, but if the crime is drug deals, why weren't they arresting the drug dealers and leaving the "loiterers" alone?

This injustice came to mind today when news broke that Milwaukee was trying to bully the players of Pokémon Go into paying for permits to enter the parks to chase down Pocket Monsters. Apparently, the nice weather this weekend and the addition of 80 new potential targets for players of the game resulted in huge crowds going to the park and loitering around.

Oh, and leaving a ton of trash. Shades of *Alice's Restaurant*; more on that later.

Milwaukee apparently wants somebody to pay for cleaning up the mess left behind by Go players (or maybe the city just sees a chance to abuse a potential source of revenue). If the concern is too much trash, perhaps they simply need more trash cans. If people leaving trash on the grounds is a problem, by all means post a few more signs threatening people with tickets for *littering*. However, does trying to chase people out of the parks make any sense? Don't we want people out in the open and sharing space and time with each other? Isn't that why we have parks?

Are we really going to have to fight the generation gap all over again? I hope not (and if so, I promise I am logically still 18 years old, even though I may well be physically older than that).

WHY IT SEEMS NOBODY CAN "FIX" HEALTH CARE IN THE US

One of the big promises made during the 2016 Presidential campaign was the promise of the Republicans to repeal and replace Obamacare. It was held up as a high priority, and bills starting implementation of the repeal were in place even before they inaugurated Trump. At the moment, it appears that the administration is doing their best to distract us from Health costs by focusing on taxes and immigration and terrorism. Looking at the problems they face with dealing with Obamacare illustrates why that might be a good path for them to follow.

According to the Milliman Medical Index, the total average medical costs for a family of four in 2016 was estimated to be $25,826. That is the total cost of medical care: premiums, employer contribution, deductibles, and coinsurance. The last time I checked, most of us could not afford over $2,000 a month for health care. The disturbing part of that number is that it only includes employees who have health care coverage at work—meaning that we have pre-selected people who are actively at work, a group that will tend to be a better class of risk than the general population.

Meanwhile, 1 in 6 Americans picked up a medical plan last year for a cost of $100 or less (based on their income). This group of new insureds is primarily the 20 million Americans who could not afford insurance either because of their low incomes or existing expense levels. Because

Obamacare covers pre-existing conditions, many of those covered under these plans have significantly worse health and higher health costs than the general population. In addition to subsidized premiums, those covered in this manner also have reduced cost sharing: lower deductibles and coinsurance. For those making less than about $17,236 a year, this means $0 in deductibles and a maximum annual out of pocket cost of only $1,000. Since the cost for a family of four covered in this manner is no doubt even higher than $25,826, this means that money from federal taxes is easily providing subsidies of over $25,000 a year to these families.

It is no wonder families making less than $35,000 a year love Obamacare—they are guaranteed coverage they could not get otherwise and they will not have to pay much for it. Meanwhile, families making more than that have seen their deductibles and coinsurance costs skyrocket, and at the same time, their premiums have gone up as well.

The only group that seems neutral about Obamacare are those who did not sign up for coverage because they are in good health (mostly the young) and it was too expensive for their income level—and now they have been "saved" from paying the penalties (taxes?) for not signing up for health insurance. Of course, any actual health emergency will be disastrous for them.

In short, as a nation, we are now using perhaps 15-20% more health care and paying for it through federal funding rather than premiums and co-payments (although those have gone up as well). If we succeed in covering everybody, we will also no doubt get an explosion in utilization of health care, immediately making it clear that we don't have enough doctors and nurse-practitioners . . . I have not noticed anybody paying attention to increasing the supply of medical care to meet the increased demand that any increase in coverage will cause.

People who have coverage at work are now paying a lot more in both premiums and copays, and people who have almost free health insurance eye any changes with the suspicion that they are losing a benefit that they now feel they deserve.

Covering people with pre-existing conditions is a challenge as well: 66% of our health care expenses go to take care of 10% of the sickest people; how can any plan cover that cost unless everybody is forced to buy health insurance? The cost of covering that sliver of the population would be twice the cost of covering everybody else, meaning many thousands of dollars per month. Lowering the cost of insurance for people with pre-existing conditions requires substantially raising the cost of insurance for everybody else. Ouch.

Where do we go from here? Anything we do hurts one group or the other, and taking nearly free health care away from those who have it now probably isn't going to happen. The only suggestion I see as viable is something along the lines of Medicare For All, with sliding premiums based on income levels and Advantage plans that fill in gaps for people who can afford to pay extra.

Anyone for Single-payer with concierge and copay coverage at an additional cost?

It is not likely that the Republicans can enact something along those lines, but then nobody expected Nixon to normalize relations with China, either.

HOW THE LAWS OF ROBOTICS
CAN HELP WITH THE SEPARATION
OF CHURCH AND STATE

A discussion with John W. Campbell (editor of Analog Magazine) led Isaac Asimov to delineate the three laws of robotics:

- A robot may not injure a human being or, through inaction, allow a human being to come to harm.

- A robot must obey the orders given it by human beings except where such orders would conflict with the First Law.

- A robot must protect its own existence as long as such protection does not conflict with the First or Second Laws.

The basic idea of the laws was that it made little sense to build robots that could go berserk and hurt humans (or evolve into Skynet and try to eliminate humans or take away their seats on planes). A zeroeth law was eventually established independently by the robots. One short story even suggested that a robot could ignore those laws to protect another robot that it considered its child. Numerous short stories and novels followed that relied on these laws or examined how they would function in practice. One story remains fresh in my memory nearly sixty years after I first read it, **Runaround**. A robot on Mercury is ordered to enter the sun-side of Mercury to get some selenium that the colonists need (this was back when our understanding of Mercury's rotation was inexact and humans still had intentions of colonizing space). After a human gives him orders to follow (Second Law), the robot tries to get the ore. When it (he?) gets in the extremely hot area of the planet, it becomes clear that continuing on that path will result in destruction, so the robot returns to the cooler part of the planet (Third Law). The decision the robot's positronic brain makes is that the robot will be destroyed and possibly be unable to complete its mission. Once the robot is safely outside of the heat, the sequence repeats itself since the heat no longer threatens the robot. The robot ends up running back and forth, unable to decide what to do. Any robot that I built would have a positronic brain smart enough to go back to the humans for advice, but this was clearly an early robot (look up **R. Daneel Olivaw** for an example of a more advanced robot). The robot's problem arises because the Second Law and Third Law are so close in importance. If a human had been trapped in the sunny sunshine and about to die, the robot would have risked certain destruction and rescued the human since the First Law is so important compared to the other two laws. In the story, this trick is actually the way the problem was resolved!

It might be nice if the Founding Fathers had drafted our Constitution with an eye towards the three laws. The constitution seems to be the First Law, with the Bill of Rights trying to spell out some of the protections of citizens that were not spelled out in the original document. In place of a positronic brain, we have the Supreme Court deciding the relative weights of the various pieces and parts that make up our laws. Since the tenth amendment has been beaten down almost into non-existence, it appears that Federal Laws always trump State Laws, but in any case, we live by the Constitution and its protections as the ironclad first laws.

Flashback to the present, when a law passed in 2012 in Missouri allowed non-profit organizations that had playgrounds to apply for the installation of recycled rubber tires to replace the pebble-infested grounds that often led to injuries. We can only hope that Missouri had enough sense to upgrade all the public-school playgrounds already, and that possibly, the law was passed to do something with left-over rubber tires. Only 44 non-profit groups applied for the help, but the state only awarded 14 of them improved playgrounds. I am not sure why the state did not believe that protecting **all** its playgrounds was a correct use of taxpayer money, but at least they allowed non-profits to apply for help. The state devised a ranking system, and a church that had a school playground came in fifth. The church's playground was skipped over because of a state law that prevents the state from spending money to support any church. Apparently giving churches exemptions from property taxes is not considered spending money, perhaps because the state feels that sort of support to all non-profit organizations is acceptable.

The conflict is similar to the one our poor little robot faced: is it more important to protect the children of the great state of Missouri or more important to avoid the possibility of being construed as supporting a religion. I am pretty sure that protecting the kids should win out in this case, and in many respects, the point is already moot—outside sources raised the money and the church's school playground now has its rubber linings. The case is still now in front of the Supreme Court, and the implications of a ruling can be important to all our futures. A narrow ruling would allow this case and no other to be affected; a wider ruling would open the door to paying for school books and lunches and oh! The whole question of vouchers supporting religious schools could be settled now instead of five to ten years from now.

Meanwhile, Missouri, please take care of the other playgrounds that weren't in your top 15.

SECTION 4:

TELEVISION AND MOVIES

Okay, so the real problem seems to be dealing with the cable companies, but there are a few other annoyances when dealing with the media.

THE ATTACK OF THE EMPTY CUPS

Last night was New Year's Eve, and on almost every network channel, there was a special countdown show that had live partiers on display. Many of them were holding cups and drinking, which made them significantly different from almost everybody you see on television. Sure, there are lots of people holding cups that they seem to drink out of on almost every show, but all those cups have one thing in common: there is no liquid in cups on television.

Ever since I first noticed this phenomenon, I have been unable to keep up with the plots or dialog when somebody picks up or carries a cup because I am too busy watching the cup and the person carrying the cup for the proof that the cup is empty. The hand carrying the cup has too easy a time waving around the cup, or the cup tilts too easily, or, well, after months of watching, I have gotten really good at being the first one to exclaim, "Empty!"

I get why they do not want cups of hot coffee on the set, and nobody ever wants to drink room temperature milk, but would it be that hard to fill the cup with water or water with a splash of food coloring so the cups have the right weight and handling them looks right?

I can understand not wanting to drink from the cups for multiple takes, but it should be easy to put the cup up to their mouth and simply not swallow the water. However, if they are not going to fill the cups with liquid, they should at least glue something in the bottom of the cup to give them some heft so the actors do not wildly wave the cups around.

White Styrofoam cups are probably the most common disposable cup in use, but red solo cups are probably the most common disposable cup in use on college campuses. Robert Hulseman, the inventor of the solo cup, died at age 84 near the end of 2016, yet another victim of a year most of us would like to simply forget. The original cups came in a lot more colors, but red seems to have won out over time.

HOW OLD IS A SENIOR?

I never really paid much attention to discounts for being a senior, mostly because I was not one, but a sign on a local movie theater window caused me to pay some attention.

The first time I had a feeling that I might actually be getting old was back in the nineties when I was not even fifty yet! Bevie and I had traveled to Salt Lake City to meet with some mostly nice folks who wanted me to move there and work in their home office. The company had recently acquired the company I worked for in Florida and wanted me to bring some computer and/or actuarial magic to the West. The company put us up at one of the suite hotels that featured a free breakfast buffet. We had grabbed some food and sat down at one of the tables that were in front of a television that was set up in the eating area so we could watch MTV videos while we ate. A well-meaning young woman (okay, she was almost a kid) came over and very deferentially asked if I would like her to turn on the news. Really? Um, no. Videos are fine. She backed away and wandered off, leaving me feeling a decade older.

While I did not move to Salt Lake City permanently, I did stay there long enough to fix up some of the company's computer files. About a month into my trip, I went to see the *Sixth Sense* and was hungry when I got out. A block or two away was a Burger King, and I went in and ordered a hamburger of some sort. Without even asking, the young woman at the counter gave me a senior citizen discount. I could have questioned her, but didn't want to embarrass her (or give back the extra quarter), so I simply wandered off chomping down on the burger and, again, feeling older. On the plus side, they did give me a burger that was never steamed with pickles and left off the cheese.

During my stay in Salt Lake, I also saw the movie, **SLC Punk**. That was enough to convince me that my problem was not that I looked a few decades older than I felt—there had to be some way youngsters in Utah are convinced that anybody who looks older than thirty or so must be treated as an elder, er, senior.

Jump forward a few decades, and now I am old enough to feel entitled to senior discounts. There has been a change in the treatment of seniors. No longer do cashiers question if you are old enough for a discount, now it seems you must demand the discount—and in many cases, it is a secret discount! That is right, I can stand at the front door of our store and see a fish place and a department store that each offer discounts all the time, but there are no signs posted for the discounts and you have to ask for them. Fortunately, nobody has ever asked for proof, but that is probably just because Utah branded me a senior for life. If you are old enough (or branded for life), be sure to start asking people if they offer discounts to seniors.

Meanwhile, back to our local movie theater in the mall. Recently, they posted a sign:

> Senior Discounts are for ages 60 and up, NOT for ages 55 and up

The sign does not indicate that this is a change, only a clarification. My first thought was that the theater must be having cash flow problems to question **anybody** who is still willing to pay the exorbitant price movie tickets cost now, so I went and visited_SeniorDiscounts.com_and checked up on movie discounts. It turns out that the most common age for discounts is indeed 60, but some chains offer them at ages as high as 62 and 65. A few chains in the Midwest have discounts at 55, but since we only have one movie theater in town anymore (see my previous comment on ticket prices!) we should probably consider ourselves lucky to have discounts at all.

WHY CLOSE ENCOUNTERS IS NUMBER ONE ON THE LIST OF FILMS I WILL ALWAYS HATE

Over the years, I have seen many movies. I grew up on Long Island in the fifties and sixties, with access to eight or nine television channels at a time when most cities were lucky to have three, so I got to see a different movie every day if I was in the mood. In addition to that, when I was single in the seventies, I went to virtually every movie that came to Nashville (even though I often walked or took a bus since I did not have a car for the first part of the decade). In the nineties, I lived in Atlanta and had a movie pass, so Bevie and I saw many, many more movies than anybody except professional movie critics. There have been movies I did not like very much, and maybe even one or two movies I walked out of before they ended, but one movie earned my permanent, perpetual hatred forever: **Close Encounters of the Third Kind**.

The movie came out around Thanksgiving in 1977, and it was a major success. You have probably even seen it, and will never look at a pile of mashed potatoes the same way again. Steven Spielberg did not feel that the movie was ready for release at that time, and wanted to wait until Summer, 1978, but Columbia was hungry for a successful film in 1977 and pressured him until he relented and released the film. That is not why I hate it.

The film lost out in the Hugo Awards to **Star Wars**, and as far as I am firmly concerned, it serves them right for what **Close Encounters** did to my budget for years.

There were special, very LOUD sound effects that you could even hear in the lobby while you waited to see the movie (because it was usually sold out and you had to wait in line to see it at all). In fact, the Academy even gave the film a special award for sound editing, and that is certainly not why I hate the film.

The film had a great series of promotional ads and did extremely well at the box office, so well that Columbia gave Spielberg another 1.5 million dollars in 1979 so he could finish the film the way he wanted and re-release it in 1980. That is not why I hate the film.

As part of the re-release deal, Columbia required that Spielberg add a scene where the audience got to see the inside of the big ship. Spielberg did not want to do that, but he added an inside scene, added some more footage, removed other footage, and ended up with the Special Edition version of the film. Sounds a lot like somebody playing around with Star Wars many years later, but that is not why I hate the film.

In 1998, Spielberg edited the film yet again, creating the Collector's Edition. This time around, he played around with a few scenes and finally removed the interior shots of the ship (because he seems to have not wanted that in his film). The appeal to collectors' pocketbooks is not why I hate the film.

No, the reason for my hatred of Close Encounters is related to one of the first times I remember being bitten by inflation! Up until Close Encounters, local movies in

Nashville were $3 after 5 pm and only $1 for the earlier matinees. Since I got off work at 4:15, I could easily get to the cheap matinees. I got to see a lot of films (and let's put that in perspective: my job in 1970 paid a whopping $2.75 an hour, so money was a lot harder to come by than it is now). **Close Encounters** apparently required special sound system installations (something more than 1974's **Earthquake**) and theaters responded by raising the price of admission to $3.50 at night and (horrors!) $1.50 for the matinees. Within months, every theater in town raised their admission prices for the matinees to $1.50 whether they raised their primetime prices or not. This price increase cost me a massive amount of money even before the rapid increase in the cost of gasoline drained our pocketbooks faster than you can say "inflation!"

A VALENTINE'S MOVIE DATE

Because I have the store to run, Bevie and I rarely get to the movies together anymore. Fortunately, there's a grandson around to give her an excuse to see cartoon movies and a son that she used to get to movies with almost weekly. For Valentine's this year, I decided to offer to close the store early and take Bevie to a movie. She, in turn, made dinner and some brownies, a good trade as far as I was concerned.

The films at our one and only movie theater that week gave us only a few choices:

Fifty Shades Darker. No, just no. Our son (Keith) got dragged to this film over the weekend, and was one of maybe three men in a very crowded theater. There's a selfie of him taken by his girlfriend that shows an air of desperation, and I was pretty sure he was looking for an exit from the theater. I trust he knows he will probably have to see the third film as well (they filmed it in the afternoons while they filmed **Darker** in the mornings, so it is inevitable that the film gets released). Bevie was not interested in this film either, so I did not have to sit through it.

The Lego Batman Movie. Bevie has been watching the Batman cartoons on demand and/or Netflix lately, and the Lego movie is probably close enough to a cartoon that she wants to see this film as well. There is still a possibility that she can see the movie with either a grandson or one or more of Keith's girlfriend's daughters, so it seemed best to give this a pass as well.

Rings. "First you watch it. Then you die." Bevie is the ultimate horror film fan, and even she was confused by the first **Ring**, so she was not too excited about this sequel. Whew, dodged a bullet . . .

A Dog's Purpose. Okay, I admit it, I cried when Old Yeller died, but I was what, eight years old at the time? I have watched Bevie snarl and turn off previews for **Marley And Me** enough times to know better than to take her to a movie where they kill a dog. Which makes it almost surprising that she wanted to see another sequel that was playing:

John Wick Chapter Two. In the first Wick movie, somebody steals John's car and kills his dog right at the start, so Bevie sat there jumping up and down waiting for John to kill the murderer (and get the Mustang back). I am almost certain that when she watched it the second time (and third and fourth times as well) she simply left the room or fast-forwarded through the part where the dog dies, so that she could watch him kill about 80 baddies. It is probably not a spoiler to anybody that John kills a lot more people in the second film (over 120), but no dogs get hurt (although the Mustang looks a little worse for wear). The ending, naturally, left Bevie hoping for Chapter Three as soon as possible.

Since Bevie declared it "The Best Valentine's Date Ever," I probably picked the right film, but then, that left me only have 12 months to figure out how to top this year's date.

CUTTING THE CORD—PART ONE

Do I like paying the cable company over $200 a month for cable, phone, and the Internet? Of course not.

I first got cable television when I moved to Knoxville, Tennessee in 1979. It was not much, we simply got a box on top of our television that had about a dozen buttons on top. Each button would let us get to a single station. The connections went to the major networks as well as the USA network, Nickelodeon, and a few forgettable channels that weren't available except on cable. It should not come as much of a surprise to anybody that my favorite part of that was the show Pop Clips on Nick that showed videos. Eventually, that show was turned into MTV, which (as you may have heard from the elderly) showed nothing but music videos 24 hours a day. I promise, some things *were* better back in the old days even if we had to walk uphill both to and from school in driving snow.

When I moved to Evansville, Indiana, cable had not yet reached my new home, and all I could watch was broadcast television. Within days, I felt like Scarlet O'Hara, holding up a cut cable and crying out, "I swear I will never go without cable again!"

After that cable had seemed to follow everywhere I went, and the number of channels expanded dramatically. Even better, in the past decade or so, we got high def channels and, wonder of wonders, the ability to record shows so we could watch them later. At first, it was nice to be able to time-shift shows so it did not matter when I got home late; I could always watch shows when I had time. Better yet, when two (or three) shows I wanted to watch were on at the same time, I could record them both and not miss any of them.

And then they added a fast forward button on the remote. The world changed. Not only was I freed from watching shows live, but now I could skip commercials and watch an hour show in 42 minutes. Television was suddenly almost as good as XM-Radio, maybe even as good as SiriusXM-radio became later.

In addition to recording shows I wanted to watch, I also recorded hours of music videos from the few channels and time slots where they still existed. I recorded news shows and watched them in ten minutes or less, scanning for stories I cared about and skipping the other stories. We could record movies off the premium channels and watch them instead of renting movies. Bevie recorded and watched horror and SciFi channel shows I would never watch and she could watch them while I was at the store.

CUTTING THE CORD—PART TWO

The ability to watch shows (content) has been been changed in the past few years. Our cable box now allows us to record at least five shows while watching a sixth, and we can record about 100 hours of high def programming before we run out of space. We can set up to record only new episodes, and if we miss one (say, if a tree literally cuts our cable line) our box automatically keeps track of the shows it couldn't record. The box then leaves a line to allow us to watch the show on demand—with commercials we can no longer fast forward past (yes, there's a workaround, but it's a nuisance and I'm in no hurry to let the cable company know about it). More likely we will simply search for later airings (commonplace for the USA network and some other cable networks) and re-record missed shows. We even have a remote that you can talk to when you want to search for something, but that is more the way Bevie searches for shows (I am still happier with text controls).

We have a smart television that allows us easy access to Amazon and Netflix (but not YouTube anymore, Google killed that app), and although our cable box has a way to connect to Netflix, the direct internet connection seems to have a better picture and much better sound. There are a few shows I cannot watch without spending more money with other online companies, but so far, that does not seem worth the money.

Our kids, not quite able to spend over $200 a month on cable, are dealing with Roku boxes and streaming shows from the web, but they may soon run into streaming limits. An example of the surprise that's coming? Our carrier has silently implemented a 1 Gigabyte monthly streaming limit, after which "additional charges" will occur.

Hulu now has a mostly-free option for a few dollars more, and many other networks are now streaming online for modest fees, but many of them still have commercials you really can't avoid even by paying extra. No thanks.

What we really need is a way to pick and choose which networks we want and pay a flat fee directly to them for on demand, commercial-free content combined with a flat fee, unlimited streaming internet connection. Since there is no competition where we live (only one available ISP), that is not likely to arrive any time soon. Even a la carte selection of channels on cable would help since we are forced to pay for sports and religion and shopping channels we never watch (and an ever-increasing number of "music channels" that don't often play music videos . . . sigh).

Am I happy with paying over $200 a month for cable? No. Am I happy with what I get for that? Sadly, yes. Will I be cutting the cord any time soon? Not a chance.

Would I pay more if cable added a music channel at an extra charge that played music videos from the 50s to the 80s? Of course. More on why that does not happen another time (watch for *The Other Day the Music Died* down in the music section of the book).

TWELVE OTHER TIMES THEY READ THE WRONG CARD FOR BEST PICTURE

The morning after the Academy presented the Oscars this year, the big news was all about the mix-up in one of the big awards. Instead of announcing **Moonlight** as the recipient for Best Picture (we do not announce winners anymore, just recipients) they announced **La-La Land**. Fortunately, somebody had the presence of mind to stop the ceremony and redirect the trophy to the correct collection of creators, but more than a few times in the past the wrong card was read, and nobody corrected the mistake. Not ever.

I am here to fix that for the Academy. The errors are listed in chronological order since I would be here for days deciding which mistake was the worst if I tried to list them as a top twelve.

Originally, there were ten nominees for each category, but that led to the kinds of problems the Academy members faced when deciding on a winner in 1939:

- Gone With the Wind

- Mr. Smith Goes to Washington

- Of Mice and Men

- Stagecoach

- Wizard of Oz

Moreover, that is only **half** of the nominees. Doesn't matter who won that year, movie goers were the winners. Starting in 1944, the nominee list was narrowed down to only five entries, although in 2009 the list was expanded back to ten since politically correct films were filling up the list before films that attracted an audience got nominated (perhaps contributing to the declining ratings for the Oscar telecasts). However, back to today's list of mistakes at past Oscar award programs:

- 1941: **How Green Was My Valley** over **Citizen Caine** (which was came in third since it was also behind **Blossoms in the Dust**).

- 1946: **The Best Years of Our Lives** over It is **A Wonderful Life**. The anti-Christmas feelings bled into 1947 when **The Bishop's Wife** and **Miracle on 42nd Street** also lost to the politically correct film, **Gentleman's Agreement** (but that was a valid choice, so the latter two Christmas movies do not get to be on our list).

- 1948: **Hamlet** over **The Treasure of the Sierra Madre** (home of "We don't need no stinking badges").

- 1952: **The Greatest Show on Earth** over **High Noon** (and **Shane** lost to **From Here to Eternity** the next year, keeping two of the best Westerns ever out of the winners, er, recipients circle).

- 1971: **The French Connection** over **A Clockwork Orange**. Perhaps if the original release of the latter had been cut down to an R earlier instead of being released with an X-rating, its card might have been handed over to the presenter.

Alternatively, maybe this was blowback over **Midnight Cowboy** winning in 1969 with an X-rating and movie theater owners paid off somebody to prevent a repeat of the problems that caused.

- 1977: **Annie Hall** over **Star Wars**. Words fail me.

- 1981: **Chariots of Fire** over **Raiders of the Lost Ark**. Oh, the humanity of it all . . .

- 1982: **Gandhi** over **E.T. the Extra-Terrestrial**. Okay, I see a pattern now . . .

- 1996: **The English Patient** over **Fargo**. I have not noticed anybody turning **The English Patient** into an acclaimed television show.

- 1999: **American Beauty** over **Toy Story 2**. Oh, wait, the Toy Story franchise was not even nominated until 2010 when three came in eighth (because, you know, animated film) so this is only a top eleven.

- 2002: **Chicago** over **The Lord of the Rings: The Two Towers**. At least the Academy corrected itself in 2003 when **The Return of the King** won.

- 2009: **The Hurt Locker** over **Avatar**. Sigh. This made us all blue.

Since 2010, the Academy has mostly been nominating films I still haven't seen (and don't intend to see) so the list has to stop there. Someday, I will have to follow up this list with a list of the times the wrong card was read for best song from

85

a motion picture, even though that is like shooting fish in a barrel.

OOPS, COMCAST DID IT AGAIN

Customers looking to "cut the cord" with their cable company to save money have usually done so by switching from using the cable company to streaming video over the Internet. Streaming means signing up for relatively cheap alternatives like Netflix and Hulu and using either a smart TV or a device (such as a Roku box) that gets between their Internet connection and their TV. Until recently, this was not difficult or expensive, and no doubt was driving down cable company revenues. Fortunately for the cable companies, consumers usually do not have any viable alternative for picking up the Internet other than the cable company. Where competition exists (hello, Google Fiber— where are you when we need you?) this resulted in very high quality, very cheap alternatives to a cable box and hideous monthly fees.

Until now.

COMCAST, which usually has a monopoly in your neighborhood if they have a wire to your house, recently announced that they were now going to limit Internet traffic to your home to only one terabyte per month (that is a thousand gigabytes), with extra charges when you exceed that limit. It was a stealth announcement in only certain cities, but unless you were paying attention, you did not notice at all. They claim that this limit is sufficient to cover most Internet usage for most customers and that only a handful of people "abusing" their Internet connection would have to pay higher fees for exceeding that limit.

At a time when most cell phone plans are rapidly becoming unlimited usage thanks to the cutthroat competition! A cynical person might think that this kind of charge is being put in place to make it uneconomical to stream video over the Internet instead of using the increasingly expensive cable boxes.

Let's do the math on the streaming usage. From Netflix: "You can adjust the quality of Netflix video playback to conserve your Internet data consumption." Netflix playback settings:

- low is .3 GB/hour,

- high def is .7 GB/hour,

- ultra-high def is 3-7 GB/hour [Xfinity does not support UHD yet, so that is out]

Most of us do not have UDH (4K) televisions yet, so we might think we are looking at .7 gigs per hour, but COMCAST (er, Xfinity) has their own estimates:

> Netflix estimates about 1 GB of data per hour for each stream of standard definition video, and up to 3 GB per hour for each stream of HD video

Not sure how the numbers change so quickly from one source to another, but I am pretty sure COMCAST is using their own numbers rather than the Netflix numbers, so that brings us to 300 hours a month of HD television without paying extra. Ten hours a day does not sound like too much, but if your household has the typical 3 or 4 televisions streaming simultaneously (got kids?), you can use that up in just 2 or 3 hours each day, and run into surprise extra fees at the end of the month. Ouch! Moreover, if you are using the Internet through your computer, that streaming counts towards your limits, too. Who knows how many bytes it takes to read through your Facebook or Google news?

Because of the fear of running over the limit, I was pleased to find Netflix as an option on our cable box. After rummaging around with our remote, I found a button on one screen that said "Netflix." Clicking on that button offered to swap cable boxes with us so we could get Netflix through our cable box. I was not too worried about clicking a few buttons on two remotes and switching to use a third remote to watch Netflix (and then undoing it when finished), but this looked like a good way to reduce our internet streaming. It would also help avoid the possibility of extra charges since shows we watch through our cable box would not count towards our monthly usage limits.

Wrong again. While at the store with nothing better to do, I went and read through all the online details about Xfinity and Netflix, and found this:

> Video in the Netflix app on XFINITY X1 is streamed over the Internet. For this reason, usage of the Netflix app on X1 and all other programming and content from the Internet on X1, as well as, the Internet apps on X1 are subject to XFINITY Internet data usage policies.

Hidden away in the online fine print is the fact that even if you watch Netflix through the cable box, it **still** counts towards your monthly streaming limits! No matter that it comes from the same lines as other television viewings, or that Netflix paid an undisclosed amount of money and somehow got around Net Neutrality to get direct lines to Comcast to "fix" connection issues, Comcast is still going to limit our ability to watch unlimited streams from the Internet.

I did not order the special box. Besides, the picture and sound from streaming directly over the Internet are still superior to the picture and sound we get from our cable box. Of course, if the new box fixed that problem, I might reconsider swapping boxes.

PS—Also announced was the upcoming availability of YouTube directly through Xfinity. While I welcome that more than Xfinity can ever know, I cannot help but fear how much that will cost us in streaming points. Isn't it finally time to break the Internet monopolies coming into our homes?

SECTION 5:

COMIC BOOKS AND GAMES

I have been running a store that sells comic books, board games and card games for over 25 years, since long before being a nerd was cool. I still read a lot of the comics, wrote a lot of role-playing adventures, and was playing Avalon Hill games when my age was still single digits. No surprise that I tend to get excited when I see some of the companies who make products we sell making mistakes that seem obvious to me.

HOW NOT TO ADD DIVERSITY TO COMICS

I am treading very carefully here since this chapter is concerned with the method of change and not the **need** for change . . . if that does not upset you, read on.

In the past year, both Marvel Comics and DC Comics have attempted to add some diversity to their main characters, perhaps in hopes of not only making the comics look more like our actual population, but also to attract additional readers. While the jury is still out on whether or not this is a good thing, the approaches the companies have taken are very, very different.

DC simply rebooted their entire universe. This reboot is not the first time for such an extreme rewrite. Plummeting sales in the New 52 made the reboot necessary. I lost track of how many comics DC has had to discontinue during the past four years, but the cancellations came in groups of 6 or 8 all too often, and not very many of the 111 comics in the New 52 made it from the start to the end. A DC reboot consists of starting over again, usually throwing away everything that came before and having all-new origin stories, new first appearances, and quite often replacements for its heroes and heroines. The main reboots were the Silver Age, Crisis on Infinite Earths, Zero Hour, Infinite Crisis, 52, Flashpoint, New 52, and now Rebirth. The Rebirth storylines relating to Wally West (Kid Flash) show one way to deal with diversity.

Not surprisingly, the original Kid Flash was a white male teenager, but over time and many reboots, he grew up and took the place of the second Flash (Barry Allen). He spent much time as a member of the Teen Titans and the Titans, but when the New 52 came along, he was sacrificed and replaced with a bi-racial Wally West (II) whom you may recognize from the television show. Fans missed Wally (after all, he had been around for over 40 years), and Rebirth was kicked into gear by Barry suddenly remembering and missing Wally, and now we have Barry, and Wally, and Wally II (we initially saw Jay Garrick's helmet, but not Jay). Net result: all the characters people grew up with are still there, but DC mixed diversity in as well, and sales are up.

Marvel comics, as far as I can tell, has never really rebooted. Right at the start of the Marvel Age of Comics, Stan Lee gave us new spins on a lot of older characters without rebooting them. In Fantastic Four #4, he went to great lengths to make it clear that the Submariner in that comic was the same one who had been in comics in the 1940s. They later tied-in and explained the old Torch, the Captain America from the 1950s, and probably a lot more that I have since forgotten. Disney now owns Marvel, and in the past year or so, there have been some major upheavals in the comics. Marvel added some interesting new characters (Moon Girl and Squirrel Girl are fun reads), but many mainstays of the Marvel Universe are gone. In particular, Hulk and Iron Man have been replaced with a 19-year-old Korean male and an African-American female teenager respectively, and in each case, Marvel killed the original character. Dead. Gone. Well, maybe reduced to a brain in a case filled with some fluid, but still not completely alive. Fans who grew up with those characters or were introduced to them in the movies (I am sure all of you can name Bruce Banner and Tony Stack) can no longer read stories that feature them. Issues with the new Hulk started over at issue 1, and it was a jumping off point for most of the readers at our store. Net result: many characters fans grew up with are gone, and the replacements are not bringing in many (any?) new readers, and sales are down . . . a lot.

So, it appears DC learned some lessons from the New 52, and we can only hope that Disney, er, Marvel, learns those lessons quickly as well.

HOW BLIZZARD TAUGHT ME TO
HATE THE WORLD OF WARCRAFT

For years, anybody who walked into the store could see I was busy doing something on my computer, and most people know that I was usually playing World of Warcraft (WoW). Playing computer games is nothing new to me; I previously spent enormous amounts of time with the online text game **Gemstone**, and I have been playing WoW since vanilla (the name players gave the first version of WoW). The most obvious proof of this is my stable of alts in the game. On my primary server, there are 37 alts that are level 100 or higher in clumps of six or more per server. On five other servers, there are ten more alts scattered about who are simply old memories of better times that refuse to die. And that does not count my other two accounts. That large number of alts was the result of a lot of play time, and most of it was fun, in part because I was in excellent guilds. The most recent expansion, however, has given me the cold shoulder, and I feel the need to share my misery over the loss of one of my life's longest companions with the release of the newest expansion, **Legion**.

The massive online multiplayer game has helped kill endless hours of boredom at the store. When each new expansion came out, I would usually focus on leveling one of my alts (usually a different one for each expansion) and then spend time leveling all the rest. This process was made easier by getting the ability for the alts to fly. Sadly, Blizzard seems to think that letting players fly makes the game too easy, so they have done everything they can to all but take that ability away from players. Grounded alts is one of the problems I have with the game now, but there are others that are just as important.

- Blizzard seems to think that making it difficult to move around is an important feature of the game. The ground layout is designed to make it difficult to travel from one place to another. Perhaps they think it is fun to make players have to memorize routes. I feel something is wrong when the only way to reach a goal that is on the map is to start up an unmarked trail that is nearly half-way across the world. Players are usually forced to go to outside websites to look up the coordinates of the start of the trail. Blizzard carefully placed rivers, canyons, mountains, elites and other obstacles in the path between where players are and where they need to be, and that serves no purpose other than to confuse travel and slow things down. Some of us had mounts that could run across water, and Blizzard attempted to make those mounts not work in Legion, but customer outrage brought them back. I find the inability to travel more than slightly frustrating. I do not mind waiting to fly until after we level at least one alt to max level, and that leads to another problem.

- Blizzard hates that we can fly, and doesn't want us to. They have tried several times to announce no flying in new expansions, and each time, they have been forced to back down. For a few expansions, we could buy flying for low-level alts, but then Blizzard limited flying to alts that reached max level and paid a huge fee in **Mists of Pandaria**. And then it got serious: forced to implement flying when they did not want to, Blizzard instead erected a long series of requirements for flying. Reputation grinds, exploration requirements, quest completion requirements, even requirements related to finding hidden "treasures" that were unrelated to leveling in any way were the new obstacles to flight.

- Even with maps, locating the large number of required treasures was a challenge. Some of the treasures also required us to take part in moving around on platforms as if we were in some Nintendo jumping game. I grew up long after Nintendo came along, and have little patience for that sort of nonsense. WoW is a role-playing game! Make me kill dragons, don't ask me to jump rocks and walls over and over again while dodging things trying to knock me down just to reach a goal! In Legion, there is even one group you need to get reputation with that seems to be interested in nothing but this sort of game.

- Blizzard added Mythic dungeons to WoW. Unlike regular dungeons or raids, there was no way to queue for these new dungeons, making it nearly impossible for casual players like myself to get into them. While I could ignore PVP and pet battles and timed dungeons, Blizzard required the Mythic dungeons for professions and the completion of some questlines. Moreover, speaking of professions . . .

- Professions have become significantly more difficult to level, have few useful rewards, and even require going through Mythic dungeons. In the past, I could have alts level professions while my main leveled up, but that is not even a possibility now.

- Blizzard does not seem to accept that some of us do not want any PVP ever. At the start of the expansion, alts were forced into PVP areas just to start some professions. No thank you. PS: isn't it time to finally get rid of the *School of Hard Knocks* achievement?

- For a long time, we have had access to Heirloom gear that made it easier to level alts, but the gear doesn't work in Legion. The Heirloom gear had bonuses to experience that helped alts level faster, and the gear automatically got better as you went up levels. The lack of these bonuses is not even the worst part of leveling alts . . .

- The weapons in Legion make it nearly impossible to run alts. Instead of getting better weapons as drops or quest rewards, you must increase the power of your one and only weapon by constantly doing other things. While this much work is okay for a main, alts get starved because there aren't enough hours in a day to run a main and an alt. Besides, any time spent on an alt causes your main to fall behind the rest of your guild's raiders. The result is nobody wants your low-powered alts around for dungeons or raids.

- The mobs in Legion increase in level as you do, so things never get any easier. The inability to outlevel mobs makes it difficult to level healers (and some underpowered specs).

- World quests require killing mobs, but you automatically share mobs with other people that are also on the quests. While this makes it easier to complete the quests, it removes the need to group up with guild members, friends, or even strangers. The game has become much more impersonal, and it feels lonely now.

When I got my selected main to max level in Legion, the problems from there were overwhelming. I stopped playing and waited for them to implement flying. When I stopped, we did not even have a list of the requirements or a date for flying, and playing simply wasn't much fun without it. I went back for a month when flying was dropped back into the expansion, but the long reputation grinds and the difficulty of moving around drove me away again. I miss the game, but the game I miss is no longer there.

KICKED AGAIN BY KICKSTARTER

Kickstarter sounds like such a clever idea. Companies planning to release a new game (or comic, or book, or almost anything) post a description of the product, and maybe some pictures, and gamers can sign up with what amounts to a pre-order for the product. Usually, there are multiple levels of support, starting with nothing for a nominal item and increasing to optional extras for people who pay extra. There are even more extra goodies for stretch goals that come into play when enough people support a product.

Kickstarter is a wonderful way for a new or small company to fund a new game since they can sell directly to their customers and sign them up on a no refund no cancellation basis. The company can even charge shipping. By starting up this way, the company can print enough copies (but not too many), have guaranteed sales, and maybe even get their game into the hands of people that will show it to other gamers (word of mouth is probably the best way to advertise a game). Best of all (for the game company), this method of selling games completely bypasses both distributors and retailers, so the company gets up to three times as much money as they normally would.

Oh, wait, I run a comic and game store. Not good news for us. A few companies have offered special retailer support and even included special promo items in the retailer copy, but that turned out not so good. In the secondary market, it turns out customers would rather pay $200 for the consumer copy with stretch goals and optional items than shell out $100 for a retailer copy with exclusive promos but no extra items. We discovered that the hard way after buying into several retailer levels for a few Kickstarter projects and selling not a single copy of the games. Not a single copy. We have pretty much stopped even trying to sell anything that came from a Kickstarter program first (with the notable exception of Cards Against Humanity, which continues to be our best-selling game even though we must buy it from Amazon and mark it up so we can make some money on it).

The newest villain in our story is Cool Mini or Not. They have a new game on Kickstarter (NO! I am not going to name it) that sells to consumers for $100. They offered retailers copies in multiples of 6 or 9 or 12 at a 40% discount. Several of our regular customers who know that we discount comics and games that they pre-order came to us to see if we would order the game and sell it to them. Since the game is not even scheduled to ship until April 2018, the customers would be relieved of the need to pre-pay now and the cost of shipping in exchange for the opportunity to pay Indiana sales tax.

While this is not even close to the discount we usually get from distributors, and we would have to pay to ship the games, I was more than happy to offer them 20% off for their orders. Even with this discount, I would recover most of my costs with the pre-ordered copies and have a few copies left over for the store to sell. At least I was happy with the deal until I looked up the Kickstarter project and found this:

Retailers agree to not breakdown the ***** pledge bundle and resell promotional items separately.

Retailers agree to sell the ***** pledge bundle at no more and no less than US$100.

Really? So, Cool Mini or Not doesn't want our store to deal directly with our customers and offer discounts as we normally do? Instead of offering us the chance to sell their game to our regular customers, they pretty much will force the customers to buy directly from them for full price.

Okay, sell all your product directly to customers, because we will not be selling any of your product in our store. Kickstarter is just one more nail in the retail game store coffin.

A NON-SPOILER SPOILER

Admit it: there have been times you went searching for spoilers, and there have been times where you did everything you could to avoid spoilers (and got royally annoyed when somebody posted one and ruined a surprise for you).

Some spoilers are no big deal (the star on a top-rated television show is not going to die from that bullet) while others are major events ("Rosebud"—'Nuff Said). In polite company, everybody expects that spoilers will be announced ahead of time so that people can avoid them . . . today, we have a spoiler that's major, but at the same time will not spoil any specific comic (although you can start searching for it!)

This year, both DC Comics and Marvel Comics have been turning their universes upside down, with mixed results. A diversity bat has been aiming at Marvel and keeps swinging at old characters and replacing them with new, modern versions:

- Tony Stark was mostly killed and replaced by a teenaged girl who somehow built her own suit

- Hawkeye shot an arrow at Hulk, not realizing it would kill Bruce Banner, and a 19 year-old Korean became the Hulk

- Ms Marvel got promoted to Captain Marvel and got replaced with a teenaged Muslim girl

DC, meanwhile, simply threw away the misery that the New 52 had become and launched Rebirth, completely retconning their entire block of history *again*. The biggest spoiler of the year was the reveal in the first Rebirth comic that Dr. Manhattan (from Watchmen) was to blame for the New 52.

In a nutshell, back in 2013, DC published a series of comics set in the Watchmen universe that was dubbed "Before Watchmen" even though some of the storylines progressed past Watchmen. In particular, at the end of the Dr. Manhattan mini-series, we see Big Blue using lightning bolts to play with a universe of his own making — a scene that looks a lot like the cover to DC Rebirth #1. On the last page of that comic, we see Batman in his cave handling a smiley button that looks like the one that has Comedian's blood on it in Watchmen issue 1. Batman muses that he feels like somebody is watching them, but there was no follow-up on that reveal for nearly a year.

So, is the Rebirth Universe somehow connected to the Watchmen Universe? Fans have debated that, but not much evidence for it has appeared. Until a comic that came out in a few months before the Button crossover. One of the comics ended with the heroes talking about the thoughts in a villain's mind during their encounter. The thought one of them overheard was just one word: "Manhattan." It would appear that DC is now going to start explaining how the universes are tied together . . . a storyline that began in The Button series in Batman and Flash issues 21 and 22 and will continue in the Doomsday Clock miniseries.

However, back to the mention of Manhattan. Which comic? Which heroes? Which villain? Come now, that would be a spoiler, and I promised I would not spoil it.

WHY YOU WILL ALWAYS BE ABLE TO FIND WALKING DEAD #163

This week, Walking Dead #163 shipped, and it is likely you will find copies everywhere you look for a long, long time. The print run was over 700,000 (compared to "only" about 175,000 copies for the highest print run in December, Justice League/Suicide Squad #1). While Loot Crate can generate print runs in the 300,000-copy range, those are not sold through stores and don't create a problem for retailers. 700,000 copies of a comic in a store is a lot.

2017 is Image Comics' twenty-fifth anniversary, and to celebrate, the company will be shipping 25 cent comics. That in itself is not enough to push the print run of the Walking Dead into the stratosphere, but there were two kickers this month:

- For every 200 copies a retailer ordered, they got one variant cover

- For every 500 copies a retailer ordered, they got one black and white variant cover

How high was demand for those two variants? The pair is already selling for at least $150 on eBay! Not just listed for that amount, but *selling* for that amount. A little quick math shows that buying 1000 copies would cost a retailer about $125 for the comics plus (ouch!) at least about another $80 for shipping, for a total cost of only $205. Four of the variants would net $300, and there would still be three more of the baby variant to sell as well for about another $75 to $150. That looks like a profit of over $150 with negligible risk as long as the retailer either lined up customers for the variants ahead of time or sells them quickly online.

There's just one little problem—this leaves the retailer with 1,000 copies of a comic with a twenty-five-cent cover price. Given that Walking Dead comics usually sell about 75,000 to 100,000 copies, all told there are nearly 600,000 extra copies hanging around. Further, since the average store probably only sells 20-30 copies of the comic, having an extra 900 copies of a comic sitting around in the store can be a real storage headache.

No doubt retailers will be giving away copies at Free Comic Book Day for years to come, unless they simply trash boxes full of the comic. Given the current sales rate of the variants, the only real regret most retailers will have about ordering the comic is not ordering more, more, more copies.

SPOILERS: IS MARVEL AIMING FOR A COSMIC REBOOT?

Seriously, there are major spoilers ahead. If you have not read Secret Empire #1 and the recent Captain Americas and Uncanny Avengers and . . . well, almost everything from Marvel this year there are spoilers. Read those comics to catch up and then come back.

While DC comics has rebooted at least a half-dozen times, Marvel comics has never actually rebooted. Marvel continuity remains intact (in spite of time travel and crashing universes). I previously noted the dismal job Marvel was doing with diversity, and the company finally acknowledged they made a few mistakes. And it looks like Marvel now plans some significant changes later this year, most of which sound like a good idea.

First up, the Generations one-shots. Putting Peter Parker and Miles Morales together in a comic is no big deal since both are still alive and kicking, but that is where the easy stuff ends. Other comics in the special crossover include: Hulks Bruce Banner and Amadeus Cho and Mar-Vell and the current Captain Marvel. Other issues include Wolverine (or Old Man Logan?) and X-23 and Tony Stark and Riri Williams.

Each of those pairs is notable for the return of somebody who is currently dead in the Marvel Universe. Granted, unlike the Ultimate Universe where dead was dead, the return of somebody who was dead is nothing new, but the story does not end with Generations.

After the special Summer series ends, we enter the Fall with Legacy. This "event" will start with a one shot that aims to kick off reuniting Marvel with its roots. After that massive 50-page comic comes out, many of Marvel's comics will return to their old numbering system, a trick they have used before. Counting up all the Amazing Spider-Man series and adding the numbers together, when Amazing Spider-Man issue 35 or so comes out, it will be number 750 or 800 or something. Marvel did this renumbering trick a few times before, and DC comics did it on a much smaller scale (only two comics so far, Action and Detective).

The renumbering is only the start: in the future, we can expect to see stories set in legacy storyline times. The telling of untold stories from the past is nothing new for Marvel. John Byrne did a series of X-Men comics (the Hidden Years) that successfully filled in missing issues of X-Men that were covered up by reprints from #66 to #93. More recently, we had a series of Avengers comics that filled in some stories that could have happened after Captain American and three villains took over for the real Avengers in issue #16. Those comics were a good read as well (12-year-old me who read that issue back in 1963 would be smug if he got to read the new comic where the new Avengers got their butts kicked; he was never very happy about the line-up change). It appears Marvel intends to publish significant quantities of comics set in olden times.

So, how will they accomplish all that? Recent events in Secret Empire #1 give us a possible suggestion. If you have kept up with the recent build-up to that issue, you realize that the cosmic cube is a lot more powerful than we ever suspected. In particular, it appears that in the Marvel Universe, the Axis and Hydra won World War II, and it was only the use of the Cosmic Cube that bent that Universe back into the stories we have been reading all these years. The implication is that Captain America was a member of Hydra all that time, and the implanted memories were only the recovered memories that previous uses of the cube hid. Once the mini-series play out, the cosmic cube could be responsible for returning all the lost heroes and setting up the recovery of memories of lost storylines as well.

Even if things do not play out that way (just who is that old man that looks like Steve Rogers in later issues of Secret Empire?), it is important to note that we are not losing all the diversity characters Disney, er, Marvel has dropped into play lately. We certainly don't want to lose Moon Girl or Squirrel Girl, and it is clear that for now, Marvel intends to move forward with stories featuring all the old characters and all of their new characters as well, which is as it should be!

WHY COMIC STORES DO NOT HAVE THE COMICS YOU WANT TO BUY

Most comic store customers pick up their new comics every week. Our store works hard to get lists from our regular customers of the comics they expect to pick up to help ensure that we have all the comics customers want. One of my customers came in this morning and was surprised when he only had four comic books waiting for him. He proceeded to pick up four more off the shelf, and was looking for others that I had already sold out of. I hope this column helps to explain how this happens to customers.

Comic book stores have only one distributor they can order most comic books from, and they must order the comics from a catalog that comes out two months before the comics ship. Most comics come out only once a month, although both Marvel and DC have started shipping a large number of their "important" titles twice a month, and Marvel now ships some mini-series weekly (thus, a four-issue series will come out once each week in a given month).

While it may be likely that a store sells about the same number of copies of Batman or Spider-Man each month, the number of copies of most other titles customers want to buy may vary dramatically depending on storylines, crossovers, new writers, new artists, or any number of other unexpected factors. Our store tries to better predict the changes in demand by getting copies of the monthly catalogs into the hands of regular customers and getting them to:

- Sit down and read through the catalog.

- Make a list of the comics they want to pick up two months later.

- Remember to bring the list back to the store.

- Show up and buy the comics they ordered two months ago.

Growing stacks of unsold comics are probably the single most important factor that leads to the death of a comic store. The comic distributor sells comic books to stores on a non-returnable basis, which means that stores have to pay for the comics whether they sell or not. Stores have to limit the number of extra comics they order past what was ordered by their customers, so getting accurate pre-orders is important.

While this explains most of the difficulty you have browsing new comics and picking out the ones you want, there are a few other wrinkles.

Imagine that issue #1 of a new comic, the **Last Cry for Help,** is scheduled to come out in the middle of July. The monthly catalog that comes out in the last week of April will have a listing for the comic. The creators can only hope that their publisher spends some money to include pictures and plot descriptions in the catalog so that potential readers will know about it (advertising on the web usually won't happen until late June or July). Within two or three weeks, customers will have to get their lists of pre-orders to their local store, and within another week, the store will have the headache of ordering copies of the **Last Cry for Help.** If enough customers order copies, or if the creators or storyline seem attractive, the store may decide to order a few extra copies as well. So far, so good.

Two weeks later, at least six weeks before issue one comes out, the new catalog comes out in the last week of May and retailers must order issue #2 already! Most readers will be reluctant to order issue two before they get to read issue #1, so retailers are in the dark and on their own when it comes time to order issue #2.

Moreover, move forward to the last week of June, and the new catalog that contains a description of issue #3 comes out. Seriously? No sign of issue #1 yet and the cries for help are no doubt coming from the poor retailers who already must order issue #3.

Oh, did I mention late-shipping comics? Suppose instead of shipping the last week of July, the **Last Cry for Help #1** ships just two weeks late, arriving in August. Can you guess what happens in the last week of July? The catalog with the description of issue #4 arrives and retailers now face the nearly impossible task of predicting sales for that issue before their customers even see issue #1.

So if you pick up issue #1 of a comic and decide you like it, you need to tell your local comic store that you want them to order issues #2 and #3 immediately.

SECTION 6:

MUSIC

When I was only four years-old, at bedtime, my parents separated my younger brother and me so we would go to sleep. They put Jon into his bed in our bedroom, and I was put into my Dad's bed with a massive radio from the forties pumping out the music of the Make Believe Ballroom that was almost as old as the radio. I would usually fall asleep quickly, and wake up in the morning back in my own bed. That stopped working the night I turned the dial around, looking for something else, and discovered a station playing Little Richard. I got up and danced around the room, and then Jon and I got moved downstairs into a pair of bunk beds. Once we moved to a larger house with separate bedrooms for all, I received my own radio, and there has been one by my bed ever since. No surprise I was on the air in Nashville doing an oldies show in the late sixties.

THE OTHER DAY THE MUSIC DIED

Pretty much everybody has heard Don McLean's song, **The Day the Music Died**, and there's not much point in kicking that song around again (unless, of course, Don finally comes clean about what was going on with the king and the marching band). I fear the Music died a far greater death another day and nobody noticed.

To me, the best part of YouTube is the performance videos by musical guests from the fifties to the eighties. Sure, a lot of it is lip-syncing, but it is fun to watch the performances even when they are not singing or playing their instruments live.

One of the good things that came out of cable tv last year was the return of Johnny Carson's Tonight shows. We only seem to be getting them from 1972 to 1992, thereby missing the first ten years he hosted the show, but it still covers a lot of ground. One of the almost-local television stations now carries reruns of Johnny's shows both late at night and very early in the morning, and we tape the shows and put them on when we go to bed at night. We are close enough to Indianapolis to be considered local by some bureaucrat who does not have to watch the dismal signals we get, but not close enough to pick up the stations well enough to watch except via cable. Just like forty years ago, we can fall asleep while the show becomes a distant, familiar pattern. We usually watch the monologue before turning off the picture and turning down the sound. If Karnack is visiting or Joan Embry is on the show with a passel of animals, we jump forward and watch that first, then rewind and start over. Alternately, Bevie also wants to fast forward and watch the Mighty Carson Art Players when they're on the show before rolling over and going to sleep, but there aren't many of those.

When the show starts, the syndicated version pops up a standard intro and shows the list of guests and the date of the show before cutting back to the actual show when Johnny comes out from behind the curtain. The list gives us a chance to either try and stay awake and wait until a specific guest appears, or start the show over in the morning and jump/fast forward to that guest. One night Jim Stafford was on, and since (as usual) I was fast asleep before the second commercial break, I pulled the show back up in the morning to watch him sing.

Jim came on stage, strummed once on his attack guitar, and then went over to sit with Johnny. Strangely, when Jim turned to walk towards the sofa, there was no sign of the guitar. It was at that moment that I realized something: The Tonight Show reruns no longer have any music. Oh sure, we hear the band performing bumper music, but except for two episodes that seem to have slipped past the modern-day censors, there are no longer any musical guests performing on the show. The shows have been edited to remove the music, and sometimes they even remove Johnny talking with the musical guests.

Some sneaking around on the web revealed the reason: an outfit named Reelin' In the Years had acquired the rights to all the music and interviews with musical guests from the Tonight show! Not sure how they could use the name of a Steely Dan song to buy up and hide so much of our musical heritage, but fear not: they have all that footage available for licensing for a fee. Just to make it clear that we are not allowed to view any of it, they have this disclaimer on their website:

> Reelin' In the Years Productions does not supply our material to fans, collectors or other private entities.
>
> We will only send material out for legitimate projects to clients in the entertainment industry.

And it is not just the Johnny Carson show—they have also snatched up all the appearances on Merv Griffin, Red Skelton, and more and more and more.

Perhaps they can make some money with licensing from all the shows, but I cannot help believing they could make even more money if they simply charged people $5 a month for streaming access to all of their videos.

AT A LOSS FOR SONGS

It is easy to find Christmas songs. Even before Thanksgiving arrives, we have one local radio station that plays them full time, and Sirius-XM now has at least one Christmas channel year-round. By Christmas Eve, almost all the broadcast stations have started wall-to-wall yuletide tunes as well. Listening to Joan Jett blast her way through **Little Drummer Boy** or waiting for the Waitresses to find a happy ending in **Christmas Wrapping** is not exactly the traditional sounds of the season, but they help to make the season bright. Most of the songs are even joyous in one way or another. But then Christmas is over, Valentine's Day displays show up at the big box stores, and we face New Year's Eve.

Websites that had no problem ranking the top 100 Christmas songs or the top 100 Country Christmas songs or the top 100 religious Christmas songs are suddenly at a loss for songs: just try and list five or ten New Year's Eve songs in sixty seconds or less. No, not songs that were near the top of the charts on New Year's, or songs about how great next year will be, but actual songs about New Year's itself. We all immediately jot down *Auld Lang Syne*, although spelling it properly or defining those words will be tough, but after that, the list is pretty thin.

The song that comes to mind for me is **Same Auld Lang Syne** by Dan Fogelberg.

The first time I head the song, I did not hear the entire song, rather I was punching buttons on my car radio to change channels and escape a commercial and ran into just the final verse:

> Just for a moment I was back at school,
> And felt that old familiar pain.
> And as I turned to make my way back home,
> The snow turned into rain.

I did not know where the sentiment came from, but I completely understood the feeling of the song just from that short clip. Later (and often) I heard the entire song, and I am pretty sure there were at least a few times when I involuntarily shed a tear to two, not out of any lost high school memories, but out of sympathy for the sadness of the song. For some reason, about half the New Year's songs are melancholy rather than hopeful, and our narrow escape from 2016 certainly feeds that feeling.

The song is about a chance meeting with a high school sweetheart several years down the line, and it turns out the song is based on an actual New Year's Eve when Dan met with a girl he knew way back when. A writer for a local paper published details about the event in 1987:

> http://www.pjstar.com/x1101623574/Luciano-Its-a-memory-that-I-cherish

Left unconfirmed is a tale that has grown around another verse from the song:

> She said she's married her an architect
> Who kept her warm and safe and dry.

> She would have liked to say she loved the man,
> But she didn't like to lie.

The girl Dan sang about was still married at the time of their meeting, but although the meeting took place in 1975, Dan apparently refused to release the song until 1980 . . . waiting until the young lady had been through a divorce with the alleged architect so as not to interfere with her marriage.

In the early seventies, my ex-wife and I lived in Nashville. Dan was one of the music people she used to go horseback riding with on the trails west of the city. Shortly after that, his career took off, and he found other trails to frequent. He probably never wrote a song about my ex-wife . . . at least I am pretty sure he didn't.

WHEN DOES A BAND
BECOME A TRIBUTE BAND?

This morning, Fox News had a musical guest at the end of **Fox and Friends**, Foreigner. Of course, they proceeded to sing their dismal biggest success, the nearly unlistenable **I Want to Know What Love Is**. Even Bevie noticed that something did not sound quite right, and it was because somebody other than Lou Gramm was doing the vocals. Lou Gramm was the original lead singer and often co-writer of all the Foreigner hits you can sing along with or name. The new vocals were good, just not identical, and a quick trip to the web revealed an almost-disturbing fact: the only member from the hit years is Mick Jones (Lou is still active, but sings in a group called "Lou Gramm, the voice of Foreigner"). On the plus side, it was Mick that put the group together and has kept it doing live shows through countless lineup changes, so there has been some consistency through the years.

Reading about the changes Foreigner went through brought to mind groups from the fifties that broke up, reformed, and even reformed and spawned multiple competing groups. Perhaps the most significant examples would include the Coasters and the Drifters, each of which had multiple groups with the same name touring simultaneously. Eventually lawsuits were filed, ownership was established, and some members learned to tour as "x of the y," just like Lou.

The Vogues toured with a Drifters group or two, and the group name "Vogues" was eventually owned seemingly by multiple people, with groups named "Vogues" and "The Vogues" in competition with each other.

Normally, listeners associate hit songs with the lead singer. When you hear a song by Herman's Hermits, you probably picture Peter Noone singing, but Peter left the group in 1971 and an assortment of other musicians kept performing as Herman's Hermits. I saw the Peter-free group live fronted by the original guitar player. We got to listen in awe when he used a piece of cloth stuck under the strings of his guitar to produce the unique sound on **Mrs. Brown You've Got a Lovely Daughter.** It was fun to hear the true guitar work, but it was a lot more fun singing along with Peter when he toured as "Herman's Hermits starring Peter Noone."

"Which One's Herman?" indeed!

The death of Duane Allman all but destroyed several groups even though he "only" played guitar, and any number of other singers have tragically died too soon, leading to many groups touring with new lead singers. Replacing a singer or an important guitarist or keyboard player is certainly better than losing the groups completely, but still leaves us with uncertainty about accepting the new lineups. Witness the Doors, who really had no career left after Jim Morrison died.

Blood, Sweat & Tears had a meaningful change after their first album, a slew of hits with their second lineup, and a series of failed later lineups. Some people still consider the Al Kooper lineup to be the only true version of the band, but the hits all came when David Clayton-Thomas was singing lead and the hits ended when he left.

With all the band breakups and reformations, it becomes difficult to know when you have the chance to see the actual band and when you have an agglomeration of musicians that perhaps have a connection to the original band, but are otherwise little more than a tribute band. In some cases, it is not very important (who does not want to listen to Paul McCartney and Ringo Starr live no matter who is backing them up?) but in other cases it is not a good idea at all. I still cringe when I remember the sad excuse for the Buckinghams that played in a small space in Nashville back in the seventies.

Flo and Eddie (aka the singers from the Turtles) have put together a series of tours that started with the Happy Together tour in 1985 and have featured lots of pieces and parts from past groups, mostly the singers:

- Gary Puckett (no Union Gap)

- Mitch Ryder (no Detroit Wheels)

- Mark Lindsay (of Paul Revere and the Raiders)

- Paul Revere and the Raiders (without Mark Lindsey)

- Mark Farner (of Grand Funk Railroad)

- Gary Lewis (but no Playboys)

- a much better version of the Buckinghams (whew!)

- the Cowsills

- the Grass Roots

- an occasional Monkee or two

Nobody in the crowd seemed too upset that it was not the original groups, or that they all shared the back-up musicians, mostly because they usually sounded very much like what the fans expected. Mostly the fans sang along and sometimes danced in the aisles. I even got to shake hands with Davy Jones (and Bevie is still jealous!)

WHY DIDN'T I KNOW HE DIED?

In 2016, we could not help but feel helpless as music icons died one after another—in no particular order, we lost George Michael, Leon Russell, Leonard Cohen, Prince, Merle Haggard, Glenn Frey, Paul Kantner, and David Bowie just for starters. Given that Elvis and a few others kicked off modern pop music over 60 years ago, it only seems likely that the number of deaths of prominent entertainers from the fifties and sixties (and beyond) will rapidly overtake us, but last year seemed particularly cruel. Moreover, that is only looking at musicians, not all the entertainers that made their mark on the world.

Perhaps an increasing awareness of death is something that happens as you get older. Lately, it seems that almost every morning I glance at the Google Entertainment news and inevitably the website delivers another name to add to the list of ex-musicians. One death earlier this year was John Wetton. Most people who recognize him do so because he was one of the founders of the group Asia, which had a hit record with **Heat of the Moment** back in 1982. The group had the good fortune to make a few videos that got picked up by MTV during its first year or two on the air, and that helped propel Asia to supergroup status. However, it is not the first group I noticed Wetton in.

Back in 1968, I was on the radio in Nashville, doing a Saturday night oldies show, and in 1969, the station schedule moved me to the drive slot, 4 to 7 pm Monday through Friday. It was only a campus radio station at

Vanderbilt, not a commercial station, so things were a lot less structured than most radio stations. To get to one of the cafeterias before it closed at 7, I would have to leave the station five or ten minutes early, and I usually accomplished that by playing a long song. **Hey Jude**, **McArthur Park**, and **Yours Is No Disgrace** were all on the list of ending songs for my show, but when I wanted to leave truly early, I could put on **Alice's Restaurant** or **In-A-Gadda-Da-Vida** or **In Held Twas I.**

An album by a new group, King Crimson, also had two very useful tracks: **In the Court of the Crimson King** and **21st Century Schizoid Man**. The album cuts were 4 and 9 minutes long, and although I liked both songs, I liked eating dinner even more. Before I started one of those two, I could tell my listeners (both of them?) goodnight, and that way I would have time to get to dinner at the best cafeteria on campus with my meal card. The poor disc jockey who came on after me finally complained about hearing **21st Century Schizoid Man** too often, so I tried harder to rotate the final record or simply queued up a second record and asked him to start it up for me.

John Wetton was also an early member of King Crimson . . . as was Greg Lake, who died in December, 2016. Let's face it, 2016 was a terrible year for musicians.

CHUCK BERRY: EARLIEST PUBLIC SUPPORT ON RECORD FOR LGBT?

Music suffered another blow when we heard that Chuck Berry was found dead. Most of the reporting has centered around his guitar riffs and a few big hits from the fifties, but if you are not that familiar with Mr. Berry and his works, you can visit the Teach Rock website and learn about him.

While there is no mistaking Chuck's impact on Rock and Roll, I would like to focus on something we seem to have overlooked: Chuck's call-out of support to the LGBT community, long before it even had a name.

Chuck had a series of hit records from 1955 to 1959, almost all of which he wrote himself (his piano player later tried to sue for co-authorship, but perhaps he waited too long to do so). Chuck's career came to a halt at the end of that period because of a jail term that arose from alleged sexual relations with a 14-year-old girl.

Elvis erupted out of Memphis, somehow combining black music and country music and producing music that was acceptable to the mass market from the waist up, and produced a long string of hits from 1955 to 1965. After that, the British invasion that was led by the Beatles stalled Elvis' career, and he failed to crack the top ten again until 1969 (instead, Elvis concentrated on movies, and released a series of not-hits that routinely just dented the charts).

Meanwhile, back in a different world populated by Donna Reed and the Beaver, Ricky Nelson covered a few black tunes and made a few forays into country-rock and had a long string of hits from 1957 to 1964. Ricky's career also came to a halt because of the British invasion. In 1969, Ricky reappeared as the lead singer in Rick Nelson and the Stone Canyon Band and barely broke into the top forty with a country-rock cover of Bob Dylan's **She Belongs to Me**. Rick's new songs did not embrace his image from the fifties, and his career vanished again.

Promoters in the early seventies hit upon a new type of show: throw together a bunch of performances of oldies featuring the original artists and hope enough people show up to pay to see the show. One of these shows occurred at Madison Square Garden in New York City on October 15, 1971, and featured both Rick Nelson and Chuck Berry. Unfortunately, instead of Ricky, the audience was confronted with a long-haired Rick Nelson and his Stone Canyon Band, and they booed him off the stage when he tried to sing country-rock. A very poor way to treat an artist who significantly contributed to the existence of country-rock.

After that, Chuck traveled to England, and on February 3, 1972, he appeared at an arts festival in Coventry and had his performance recorded live. An album of new songs and some songs from that live performance was released, and not much happened with it.

Still stinging from the poor reception he got in New York, Rick recorded a song that turned out to be his last visit to the top ten, **Garden Party**. A few lines from the song speak for themselves:

I said "Hello" to Mary Lou, and She Belongs to Me,
When I sang a song about a honky-tonk, it was time to leave.

Someone opened up a closet door, and out stepped Johnny B. Goode,
Playing guitar like ringing a bell, and looking like he should.

If you gotta play garden parties, I wish you a lot of luck,
If memories were all I sang, I'd rather drive a truck.

The record immediately climbed the charts in the middle of the Summer; perhaps not so coincidentally, a month later, the radio started playing Chuck Berry's new single, his only number one record: **My Ding-A-Ling.** Dave Bartholomew did the original version of the song in 1952 and the Bees did a modified version retitled **My Toy Bell** in 1954. Chuck had even done a modified studio version in 1966 entitled **My Tambourine**, but nobody noticed at all. This time the live version was released, and it was a much more interesting take on the song (there are lots of live versions of the song on YouTube, but you may only be able to find the edited single here). In addition to turning the tambourine back into a ding-a-ling, Chuck talked to the audience. Before starting out he got the crowd to practice singing along, with the girls singing, "My," followed by the boys singing "Ding-a-ling." The song was suddenly very raunchy, and much more humorous, but the surprising lines he spoke in the middle of the song were a complete surprise in 1972:

I hear two girls out there singing in harmony. This is a free country, live like you wanna live, baby.

There's one guy over here singing "My," too. That's alright, bro.
Yes sir, you got a right baby, ain't nobody gonna bother you.

I have spent the morning trying to remember another pop record that had a positive message for gays and lesbians either before that record or for a long time after it, but I simply can't. It is even difficult to find many songs with a positive message for the LGBT crowd in recent times.

That same month, the radio began playing the last Elvis song to reach the top ten, **Burning Love**. After that, Chuck had one more record barely reach the top forty late in the year. 1972 had all but put an end to the recording careers of three of the most prominent recording acts of the fifties.

I saw Chuck in concert a few times in the next few decades, but each time was as part of a large rock and roll oldies show. Each time Chuck came out still looking like he should, playing guitar like ringing a bell, doing the duckwalk, and only singing his core hits from the fifties. No sign of anybody's ding-a-ling, no talking, and no interaction with the audience, just wind him up and send him out on the stage. Perhaps he simply played one too many garden parties. His early shout-out to more than one audience is now all-but-forgotten, but his musical legacy remains. Perhaps I have given you something else to remember him by as well.

BEST GIG OF THE SEVENTIES:
WARM-UP ACT FOR J. GEILS BAND

It is a long-established fact that musical groups can develop a following by appearances and tours long before they have a hit record. In today's world of overnight YouTube and Facebook sensations, it seems like success comes much easier than in the past when groups sometimes toiled for years before gaining enough recognition to be successful.

The J. Geils band was named for its guitar-playing founding member who died earlier this week. The most recognizable member was (as usual) its lead singer, Peter Wolf, and its most notable musician was the harmonica player, Richard Salwitz (aka Magic Dick). The group toured extensively during the 1970s, mostly performing their own form of blues rock (after all, they did have a harmonica as a lead instrument at times). In spite of limited record sales and chart success, the group's live performances allowed them to play almost non-stop tour dates with a very impressive list of warm-up acts. I am not sure if the group had somebody working for them who could spot up and coming acts years before anybody else or if the music the group was playing attracted musicians from future major rock and rollers, but the list of acts opening for them was impressive. I saw the group in concert at a show in the 1970s and was very impressed with the warm-up act . . . however, after J. Geils Band did four or five songs, it was all starting to sound the same, and I left early.

In 1982, rock critic, Dave Marsh and Kevin Stein published **The Book of Rock Lists**. I vaguely remember reading the book when it came out, but one list stood out that I instantly recalled with the news of J. Geils' death: the Top Ten Acts That Opened For J. Geils Band. At the time that book was written, J. Geils had not yet had their career hits (**Freeze Frame** and **Centerfold**). The list of acts that opened for them at one time or another was pretty impressive, even though the list did not contain perhaps the most successful group that opened for them (more on that later).

It turns out that in 1994, Dave Marsh and James Bernard turned out **The New Book of Rock Lists**. Instead of digging out my old copy of the first print of the book, I ordered a used copy of the newer book from Amazon to see if they had updated the earlier list. While waiting a few days for the book to arrive, I browsed around on the web and found an exciting website (well, exciting to me at least):

> http://thejgeilsband.blogspot.com/p/the-j-geils-band-tour-dates-1970-1983.html

This site lists countless dates the band played throughout the seventies and eighties. Even though the list of dates still isn't complete, it makes any list from the Rock Lists books irrelevant. Here are a few of the groups that opened for the band during 1971 (and note that the lists that follow are by no means complete):

> Emerson, Lake and Palmer, Black Sabbath, Johnny Winter, Eric Burdon and War, Procol Harum, Allman Brothers, Traffic, Fleetwood Mac, Yes, Sha Na Na, Alice Cooper

In late 1971, the band released their first successful single; **Looking For a Love,** which clawed its way up to number 39 on Billboard's Top 40 chart (so they even got to hear Casey Kasem introduce their record). And that was **after** all those groups opened for them. That single was enough of a shot in the arm that in 1972 they had another excellent run of warm-up acts:

> King Crimson, Neil Young & Crazy Horse, Yes, Billy Joel, Edgar Winter, Humble Pie, Slade, Peter Frampton, Boz Scaggs, Dr. Hook, Eagles, Loggins and Messina

The next successful hit for the group came in 1973 when **Give It To Me** reached number 30. Their first real success came when the single **Must Have Got Lost** in 1975 climbed all the way to number 12, allowing the group to run through yet another large number of future superstars as their warm-up acts:

> REO Speedwagon, Joe Cocker, Styx, Charlie Daniels Band, Bob Seeger, Rod Stewart and the Faces, Lynyrd Skynyrd, ZZ Top, Steve Miller, The Cars, Journey, Tom Petty, Def Leppard

The group had two more minor singles in 1980, *Come Back* (#32) and *Love Stinks* (#38), but their future break out into superstardom was dependent on a date that changed the music world: in August 1981, MTV was created. The small exposure that Pop Clips gave their records in 1980 was nothing compared to being seen on MTV, and in 1982, *Centerfold* went all the way to #1. On the heels of that hit, *Freeze Frame* made it up to #4. After that, of course, the group broke up (they reformed off and on beginning in 1999).

The last time I saw the group in concert was at a show in Knoxville in March 1982 when the group was touring with their two biggest hits. MTV had played a recent video that the warm-up act was touring to support, and I was interested in seeing them live. They turned in a dynamic performance, and it was amusing to watch their lead singer climb around the rafters of the stage so he could sing from on top of the largest speakers (the kind of shenanigans that Peter Wolf apparently did earlier in the J. Geils Band career). The song that they were touring in support of, **Gloria**, never hit the charts, and the group did not get a top 40 record for another two years. Even that record only got to number 33 on the charts, and it was yet another year before U2 hit number 1 singing **With or Without You**. J. Geils Band that night? They did a few of their singles, and I liked the show for a while, and then it all started to sound the same and I left early again. I did enjoy the warm-up act a great deal.

The video for Love Stinks could have made the song a much bigger hit if MTV had only started up sooner.

CAN'T WE ALL JUST SING ALONG?

Many, many years ago I was waiting in a line at a KFC, hoping for food. It was a small piece of luck that the background music in the store was something other than Muzak, and when the Four Tops came on, I naturally started singing along. The line finally moved along a little bit, and as I moved forward, I glanced at the two people behind me in line. There was a young non-Caucasian standing there with a man who appeared to be old enough to be his grandfather (time has eaten some of my memory of the day, but not the important parts).

The kid appeared to be confused that I was singing along with the song, and turned to his elder and complained that I seemed to know the song well enough to sing along. The man shook his head, and said, "It's like I keep telling you. Back in the day, we used to all be together." Given when this happened, it is likely he was referring to the sixties, a time when things like Woodstock happened, but in the present day, I fear we have even bigger hurdles to overcome.

Before cable showed up, most towns only had three or four television stations, and in most areas, there were only three main networks and maybe PBS available. As a result, a significant percentage of the population was watching any particular show, and if a show was a big hit, everybody saw it live (video tape recorders were not widespread until the middle seventies). Now there are so many choices for viewing that even hit shows have ratings that are so low the networks would have quickly canceled the shows in the past.

Radio stations were more widespread than television, especially at night. The FCC set aside AM channels between 600 and 1000 for a very limited number of clear channel stations. At night, those stations could boost their power and be heard over a wide area. Most places I have lived could pick up WLS in Chicago with ease, and I even had preset buttons in my car set to it while living in Nashville and Atlanta, and some nights I could even pick up the signal on the hills of Austin. When I was a disc jockey in the sixties, I could pull records from our playlist and play an assortment of records back to back that seems impossible now:

> Johnny Cash, Led Zepplin, Andy Williams, Beatles, the Archies, the Supremes, Blood Sweat and Tears, Country Joe and the Fish, and Judy Collins.

All those artists could be played back to back in the same hour, and nobody gave it a second thought. Stations abandoned true top 40 radio for Narrowcasting. Our choices became a plethora of radio stations that played only rap, or pop, or country pop, or oldies, or gospel, or classic rock, or some other niche designed to attract just a small but focused audience. Sirius-XM radio goes even further, allowing online listeners to tailor their listening habits to not only select one of over 100 stations, but even letting us increase or decrease the amount of Motown or bubble gum or big hits or little hits on each narrow-casted station.

And now there's the Internet. Not only can you stream only the songs you think you want to hear, but you even can select the way you get news, recipes, shopping, or pretty much anything. The ability of the web to narrowcast threatens to divide us even more, leaving us with almost no shared experiences anymore. How can we ever hope to reach the one world promise of Woodstock if modern life leaves us so hopelessly divided that we have no common ground?

Somewhere, I hope that little kid has grown up to remember how to still sing along with the Four Tops and we should all feel free to dance along as well.

AFTERWORD

Surveys show that most people don't read all the way to the end of a book . . . or maybe they just skip to the end and don't read the middle. Either way, congratulations on making it this far!

Either way, there is one last request for you: please leave a review of the book on Amazon and any other places where you think readers might stumble upon your reaction to the book. I'm already hard at work on the sequel, and will always strive to find a way to make reading my books better for the readers.

ABOUT THE AUTHOR

Rembert N Parker somehow survived growing up in the fifties and sixties and has worked numerous jobs in an effort to avoid writing for a living. Past jobs include photographer's assistant, golf caddy, busboy, librarian, disc jockey, computer programmer, actuary, talk show host, comic book store owner, and most recently university professor. From time to time he slipped up and wrote a few things that managed to get published, but most of that was simply gaming adventures for Dungeons and Dragons and other role-playing games. Several new books seem to be on their way later in 2017.

Rembert can usually be found at his comic and game store, Reader Copies. He lives near Anderson, Indiana with his wife Bevie, a dog, one or more cats, a few birds, a bunny, and assorted fish.

Thanks to an explicit pre-nuptial agreement, he never has to mow the lawn.

Made in the USA
Middletown, DE
22 October 2018